Taste_of_Home
FARMHOUSE FAVORITES

FARMHOUSE FAVORITES

TASTE OF HOME BOOKS • RDA ENTHUSIAST BRANDS, LLC • MILWAUKEE, WI

© 2021 RDA Enthusiast Brands, LLC.
1610 N. 2nd St., Suite 102, Milwaukee, WI 53212-3906
All rights reserved. Taste of Home is a registered trademark of
RDA Enthusiast Brands, LLC.
Visit us at tasteofhome.com for other Taste of Home books and products.

ISBN Retail: 978-1-61765-952-2
ISBN DTC: 978-1-61765-978-2
LOCC: 2020936337

Executive Editor: Mark Hagen
Senior Art Director: Raeann Thompson
Assistant Art Director: Courtney Lovetere
Designer: Jazmin Delgado
Copy Editor: Ann Walter

Cover
Photographer: Dan Roberts
Set Stylist: Stacey Genaw
Food Stylist: Shannon Norris

Pictured on front cover: Oven-Fried Chicken Drumsticks, p. 207;
Skillet Herb Cornbread, p. 84; Red Potatoes with Beans, p. 166; Elegant
Fresh-Berry Tart, p. 305

Pictured on title page: Best Strawberry Shortcake, p. 326

Pictured here: Chicken, Nectarine & Avocado Salad, p. 45; Cowgirl by
Jacquie Parr, p. 180; Bacon-Blue Cheese Stuffed Burgers, p. 54; Barn by
Donna Buechler, p. 5

Pictured on back cover: Bacon Corn Pancakes, p. 20; Laughing Girl by
Hillary Sphuler, p. 302; Cherry Tomato Salad, p. 57; Girl with Peaches by
Jaemor Farms, p. 148; Festive Meat Loaf Pinwheel, p. 216; Farmhouse by
Sunny Herrmann, p. 126; Blueberry Lattice Bars, p. 270

INSTANT POT is a trademark of Double Insight Inc. This publication has not
been authorized, sponsored or otherwise approved by Double Insight Inc.

Printed in China
3 5 7 9 10 8 6 4

A TASTE OF THE COUNTRY

It's time to sit back, relax and savor all of the comforting flavors the country has to offer.

From hearty breakfasts, all-American barbecues and meat-and-potato dinners to garden-fresh veggies, buttery breads and family-reunion desserts, the down-home comforts found at a farmhouse table are simply irresistible.

This keepsake collection of 142 time-tested recipes comes directly from farmhouse cooks as well as those who live in (and long for) the country. Now you can relish the specialties enjoyed in their homes—the foods they set on their tables, rely on for holidays and turn to when a sweet tooth comes calling.

Inside you'll discover all of the finger-licking staples folks crave the most. Grilled ribs slathered in sauce, roasted chicken ideal for Sunday dinner, thick savory stews and maple-glazed ham—these are the meals that deliver country goodness to any table.

You'll even find a section of Instant Pot, air-fryer and slow-cooked mainstays so you can enjoy stick-to-your-ribs favorites when time is tight.

Round out your menus with brilliant side dishes featuring in-season produce, aromatic dinner rolls, cornbread baked to perfection in a cast-iron skillet, and other classics that make every farmhouse meal extra special.

This mouthwatering cookbook simply wouldn't be complete without an amazing array of sweets shared by home bakers. Whether you need cookies, brownies or bars for a bake sale, or berry pies, layered cakes or frosty delights sure to impress, you'll find the perfect treat right here.

This extraordinary book even takes a peek into the lives of farming families with breathtaking photography, heartwarming stories and the secrets to getting the most out of country living.

So settle in for the goodness of from-scratch biscuits, crispy drumsticks, refreshing lemonade and more. With *Farmhouse Favorites*, the best of country cooking is always the special of the day.

CONTENTS

CHAPTER 1

FARMHOUSE BREAKFASTS

A hearty breakfast takes top priority in the country. See how easily farm-fresh eggs, sizzling bacon, aromatic baked goods and other eye-openers warm both the heart and the soul.

HAM & COLLARDS QUICHE

I love quiche and wanted to make something to celebrate my southern roots, so I came up with this recipe. Featuring eggs, cheese, ham and collard greens in a flaky crust, it's a complete meal.

—Billie Williams-Henderson, Bowie, MD

PREP: 20 MIN. • **BAKE:** 35 MIN. + STANDING • **MAKES:** 6 SERVINGS

1 sheet refrigerated
   pie crust
2 Tbsp. olive oil
1 cup frozen chopped
   collard greens,
   thawed and drained
1 small onion, chopped
1 garlic clove, minced
¼ tsp. salt
¼ tsp. pepper
2 cups shredded Colby-
   Monterey Jack cheese
¾ cup cubed fully
   cooked ham
6 large eggs
1 cup 2% milk

1. Preheat oven to 375°. Unroll crust into a 9-in. pie plate; flute edge. Chill while preparing filling.

2. In a large skillet, heat oil over medium-high heat. Add collard greens and onion; cook and stir 5-7 minutes or until the onion is tender. Add garlic; cook 1 minute longer. Stir in salt and pepper. Cool slightly; stir in cheese and ham. Spoon into crust.

3. In a large bowl, whisk the eggs and milk until blended. Pour over the top.

4. Bake on lower oven rack until a knife inserted in the center comes out clean, 35-40 minutes. Cover edge loosely with foil during the last 15 minutes if needed to prevent overbrowning. Remove foil. Let stand 10 minutes before cutting.

FREEZE OPTION: Cover and freeze unbaked quiche. To use, remove from freezer 30 minutes before baking (do not thaw). Preheat oven to 375°. Place quiche on a baking sheet. Bake as directed, increasing time to 50-60 minutes.

1 SLICE: 457 cal., 31g fat (15g sat. fat), 240mg chol., 766mg sod., 23g carb. (4g sugars, 1g fiber), 21g pro.

BLUE
RIBBON
WINNER

BLUEBERRY STREUSEL COFFEE CAKE

Filled with juicy berries and crunchy pecans, this all-time family
favorite coffee cake smells simply wonderful as it bakes.

—Lori Snedden, Sherman, TX

PREP: 20 MIN. • BAKE: 35 MIN. • MAKES: 9 SERVINGS

2 cups all-purpose flour
2 tsp. baking powder
¼ tsp. salt
¾ cup sugar
½ cup butter, softened
1 large egg, room
   temperature
½ cup whole milk
1 cup fresh or frozen
   blueberries
1 cup chopped pecans

STREUSEL TOPPING
½ cup sugar
⅓ cup all-purpose flour
¼ cup cold butter

1. Preheat oven to 375°. Whisk flour, baking powder and salt. In another bowl, cream sugar and butter until light and fluffy. Add egg and milk; stir into dry ingredients. Fold in blueberries and pecans. Spread into a greased 9-in. square baking pan.

2. For topping, combine sugar and flour; cut in butter until crumbly. Sprinkle over batter. Bake until a toothpick inserted in the center comes out clean, 35-40 minutes. Cool on a wire rack.

1 SLICE: 476 cal., 26g fat (11g sat. fat), 66mg chol., 323mg sod., 57g carb. (30g sugars, 3g fiber), 6g pro.

RASPBERRY STREUSEL COFFEE CAKE: Substitute raspberries for the blueberries.

EASY GLAZED BACON

Brown sugar, mustard and a little wine make bacon a bit more special in this recipe.
It's easy to prepare for weekend brunches while working on the rest of the buffet.
—*Judith Dobson, Burlington, WI*

PREP: 10 MIN. • **BAKE:** 30 MIN. • **MAKES:** 8 SERVINGS

1 **lb. sliced bacon**
1 **cup packed brown sugar**
¼ **cup white wine or unsweetened apple juice**
2 **Tbsp. Dijon mustard**

1. Preheat oven to 350°. Place bacon on a rack in an ungreased 15x10x1-in. baking pan. Bake 10 minutes; drain.

2. Combine brown sugar, wine and mustard; drizzle half over bacon. Bake 10 minutes. Turn bacon and drizzle with remaining glaze. Bake 10 minutes or until golden brown. Place bacon on waxed paper until set. Serve warm.

2 SLICES: 221 cal., 10g fat (3g sat. fat), 16mg chol., 404mg sod., 27g carb. (27g sugars, 0 fiber), 6g pro.

MORNING NAP
"We get so excited about calving season and the potential within every calf. This one had a rough start; we hand-fed him for his first few days. He never seems to mind our little cowboy, Cooper, taking a quick nap with him."
—*Kim Doggett, Pulaski, Tennessee*

FROM TOP:

RISE AND SHINE

"This bright, vibrant rainbow over the grain bins is a sure reminder of the Lord's great beauty and promise. The sky after a morning storm is a welcome pop of color."

—*Grace Westerman, Sauk Centre, Minnesota*

MAKE A WISH

"There's nothing better than blowing dandelions and making wishes with a warm breeze at your back."

—*Indra Corey, Bismarck, North Dakota*

PUFFY APPLE OMELET

With all the eggs our chickens produce, I could make this omelet every day!
It's an impressive dish that's wonderful for breakfast and light suppers.

—*Melissa Davenport, Campbell, MN*

TAKES: 30 MIN. • MAKES: 2 SERVINGS

3   Tbsp. all-purpose flour
¼   tsp. baking powder
⅛   tsp. salt, optional
2   large eggs, separated,
    room temperature
3   Tbsp. 2% milk
1   Tbsp. lemon juice
3   Tbsp. sugar

TOPPING
1   large apple, peeled if
    desired, and thinly sliced
1   tsp. sugar
¼   tsp. ground cinnamon

1. Preheat oven to 375°. Mix flour, baking powder and, if desired, salt. In a small bowl, whisk together egg yolks, milk and lemon juice; stir into flour mixture.

2. In another bowl, beat egg whites on medium speed until foamy. Gradually add sugar, 1 Tbsp. at a time, beating on high after each addition until stiff peaks form. Fold into flour mixture.

3. Pour into a 9-in. deep-dish pie plate coated with cooking spray. Arrange apple slices over top. Mix sugar and cinnamon; sprinkle over apple.

4. Bake, uncovered, until a knife inserted in the center comes out clean, 18-20 minutes. Serve immediately.

1 PIECE: 253 cal., 5g fat (2g sat. fat), 188mg chol., 142mg sod., 44g carb. (32g sugars, 2g fiber), 9g pro.

KITCHEN TIP: It's the filling in most puff pancakes that often makes them unhealthy. This recipe, however, uses just a touch of sugar for sweetness.

BACON CORN PANCAKES

Stir in crumbled bacon and a bit of corn for pure pancake perfection! I cook gluten-free,
but you can easily use regular all-purpose flour for these change-of-pace flapjacks.

—Anne-Marie Nichols, Watkinsville, GA

PREP: 20 MIN. • COOK: 10 MIN./BATCH • MAKES: 18 PANCAKES

2 cups gluten-free all-
purpose baking flour
or all-purpose flour
1 Tbsp. sugar
2 tsp. baking powder
½ tsp. salt
⅛ tsp. pepper
2 large eggs, room
temperature
1½ to 1¾ cups rice milk
2½ cups fresh or frozen corn
1 cup crumbled
cooked bacon
⅓ cup chopped onion
Maple syrup

1. Preheat griddle over medium heat. In a large bowl, combine
the flour, sugar, baking powder, salt and pepper. In another
bowl, whisk the eggs and rice milk; stir into dry ingredients just
until moistened. Stir in corn, bacon and onion.

2. Lightly grease griddle. Pour batter by ¼ cupfuls onto griddle;
cook until edges are dry and bottoms are golden brown. Turn;
cook until the second side is golden brown. Serve with syrup.

FREEZE OPTION: Freeze cooled pancakes between layers of
waxed paper in a freezer container. To use, place pancakes
on an ungreased baking sheet, cover with foil and reheat in
a preheated 375° oven until heated through, 5-10 minutes. Or,
place a stack of 3 pancakes on a microwave-safe plate and
microwave on high until heated through, 45-90 seconds.

3 PANCAKES: 318 cal., 8g fat (2g sat. fat), 67mg chol., 868mg sod.,
50g carb. (10g sugars, 5g fiber), 16g pro.

FLUFFY WAFFLES

Not only are these waffles light and delicious, but the homemade syrup
is a nice change of pace. Our two children even love the syrup on toast.

—Amy Gilles, Ellsworth, WI

PREP: 25 MIN. • **COOK:** 20 MIN. • **MAKES:** 10 WAFFLES (6½ IN.) AND 1⅔ CUPS SYRUP

2 cups all-purpose flour
1 Tbsp. sugar
2 tsp. baking powder
½ tsp. salt
3 large eggs, separated
2 cups milk
¼ cup canola oil

CINNAMON CREAM SYRUP
1 cup sugar
½ cup light corn syrup
¼ cup water
1 can (5 oz.)
   evaporated milk
1 tsp. vanilla extract
½ tsp. ground cinnamon

1. In a bowl, combine the flour, sugar, baking powder and salt. Combine the egg yolks, milk and oil; stir into dry ingredients just until moistened. In a small bowl, beat egg whites until stiff peaks form; fold into batter. Bake in a preheated waffle iron according to manufacturer's directions.

2. Meanwhile, for syrup, combine sugar, corn syrup and water in a saucepan. Bring to a boil over medium heat; cook and stir for 2 minutes or until thickened. Remove from the heat; stir in the milk, vanilla and cinnamon. Serve with waffles.

FREEZE OPTION Cool waffles on wire racks. Freeze between layers of waxed paper in a resealable plastic freezer bag. Reheat waffles in a toaster on medium setting. Or, microwave each waffle on high for 30-60 seconds or until heated through.

1 WAFFLE WITH 2½ TBSP. SYRUP: 424 cal., 12g fat (4g sat. fat), 94mg chol., 344mg sod., 71g carb. (41g sugars, 1g fiber), 9g pro.

COUNTRY APPLE-SAUSAGE HASH

I serve this versatile recipe over cheddar grits or topped with a fried egg. If you ask me,
it even makes a hearty side dish at dinner. Leftovers make a great lunch the next day.

—Crystal Schlueter, Northglenn, CO

TAKES: 30 MIN. • MAKES: 4 SERVINGS

2 Tbsp. canola oil
½ cup chopped onion
4 fully cooked apple
  chicken sausages
  or flavor of your
  choice, sliced
1½ cups thinly sliced
  Brussels sprouts
1 large tart apple,
  peeled and chopped
1 tsp. caraway seeds
¼ tsp. salt
⅛ tsp. pepper
2 Tbsp. finely chopped
  walnuts
1 Tbsp. brown sugar
1 Tbsp. whole grain
  mustard
1 Tbsp. cider vinegar

1. In a large skillet, heat oil over medium-high heat; saute onion until tender, 1-2 minutes. Add sausages, Brussels sprouts, apple and seasonings; saute until lightly browned, 6-8 minutes.

2. Stir in walnuts, brown sugar, mustard and vinegar; cook and stir 2 minutes.

1 CUP: 310 cal., 17g fat (3g sat. fat), 60mg chol., 715mg sod., 25g carb. (19g sugars, 3g fiber), 16g pro.

HAPPILY EVER AFTER

BY AMARA L. BIEDLER WESTVILLE, OKLAHOMA

Every little girl dreams of growing up, meeting her fabled farmer on his trusty tractor and riding off into the sunset to the land of chickens and eggs. Wait—that's not how it goes? Well, it wasn't like that for me, either. But it is the happily-ever-after that I'm living.

When I was 12, our family moved onto a 350-acre farm in West Virginia. Then I met a boy named Mark who swept me off my feet.

After college, Mark and I landed in Illinois with a 1-year-old, a 2-week-old, and a house with a small farm. I realized that we had room for chickens. What a neat experience it was for the kids to have chicks of their own.

Eventually, we added two more children to our family, moved to Oklahoma and settled into a house on 54 acres. We purchased goats, more than a dozen calves, piglets, ducks, turkeys and, of course, lots and lots of chickens.

After helping out with some new friends' laying hens, an idea was hatched: Maybe we could do this ourselves!

The opportunity to sell eggs to a company presented itself, and we spent a year making that a reality. We added 10,000 pastured laying hens, with the goal of Mark farming full time.

Fast forward a few years to us owning two barns full of fluttering birds. Mark is now a full-time farmer, and we have a contract with an egg company that purchases our eggs. Each pallet holds 10,800 eggs, and we usually have five to six pallets ready for pickup weekly.

Best of all, this is something we all get to do as a family: continuing to grow our farm while including our children in this future—with our chickens. Lots and lots of chickens. If that's not happily ever after, I just don't know what is.

Top: The Biedler children—Miles, Mariel, Miriam and Matthias—have been a part of their parents' farm dreams since the beginning.
Bottom: Daughter Mariel lends a hand on the family farm; Mark Biedler prepares pallets of eggs for another pickup.

BACON EGG CUPS

This breakfast dish is a fresh take on the classic bacon-and-eggs
combo. Make sure to use ovenproof bowls when baking!

—Carol Forcum, Marion, IL

PREP: 20 MIN. • BAKE: 20 MIN. • MAKES: 2 SERVINGS

4 **bacon strips**
4 **large eggs**
⅓ **cup half-and-half cream**
⅛ **tsp. pepper**
½ **cup shredded**
    cheddar cheese
2 **green onions, chopped**

1. In a small skillet, cook bacon over medium heat until cooked
but not crisp. Remove to paper towels to drain; keep warm.

2. In a small bowl, whisk 2 eggs, cream and pepper. Wrap
2 bacon strips around the inside edges of each of two 8-oz.
ramekins or custard cups coated with cooking spray.

3. Sprinkle each with half of the cheese and onions. Divide egg
mixture between ramekins. Break 1 of the remaining eggs into
each ramekin. Sprinkle with remaining cheese and onion. Bake
at 350° until eggs are completely set, 18-22 minutes.

1 SERVING: 380 cal., 28g fat (14g sat. fat), 486mg chol., 521mg sod.,
5g carb. (3g sugars, 0 fiber), 24g pro.

HONEY BAGELS

Who has time to make from-scratch bagels? You do, with this easy recipe! The chewy golden bagels offer a hint of honey and will win over even the pickiest eaters.
—Taste of Home *Test Kitchen*

PREP: 1 HOUR + STANDING • **BAKE:** 20 MIN. • **MAKES:** 1 DOZEN

1 Tbsp. active dry yeast
1¼ cups warm water
   (110° to 115°)
3 Tbsp. canola oil
3 Tbsp. sugar
3 Tbsp. plus ¼ cup
   honey, divided
1 tsp. brown sugar
1½ tsp. salt
1 large egg, room
   temperature
4 to 5 cups bread flour
1 Tbsp. dried minced onion
1 Tbsp. sesame seeds
1 Tbsp. poppy seeds

1. In a large bowl, dissolve yeast in warm water. Add the oil, sugar, 3 Tbsp. honey, brown sugar, salt and egg; mix well. Stir in enough flour to form a soft dough.

2. Turn onto a floured surface; knead until a smooth, firm dough forms, 8-10 minutes. Cover and let rest for 10 minutes.

3. Punch dough down. Shape into 12 balls. Push thumb through centers to form a 1½-in. hole. Stretch and shape dough to form an even ring. Place on a floured surface. Cover and let rest for 10 minutes; flatten bagels slightly.

4. In a large saucepan or Dutch oven, bring 8 cups water and remaining honey to a boil. Drop bagels, 1 at a time, into boiling water. Cook bagels for 45 seconds; turn and cook 45 seconds longer. Remove bagels with a slotted spoon; drain and sprinkle with minced onion, sesame seeds and poppy seeds.

5. Place the bagels 2 in. apart on baking sheets lined with parchment. Bake at 425° for 12 minutes. Turn and bake until golden brown, about 5 minutes longer.

1 BAGEL: 265 cal., 5g fat (1g sat. fat), 16mg chol., 303mg sod., 48g carb. (14g sugars, 2g fiber), 7g pro.

CHAPTER 2

DOWN-HOME LUNCHES

A busy morning on the farm calls for a refreshing lunch at noon.
Whether gathering family for a midday bite or brown-bagging it
to work, enjoy a taste of the country with these dishes.

BAKED HAM & COLBY SANDWICHES

This yummy recipe is a winner. Not only are the warm sandwiches a snap to prepare, but they smell so good while baking that no one can resist them. They're a staple at our house.

—*Sherry Crenshaw, Fort Worth, TX*

TAKES: 30 MIN. • MAKES: 8 SANDWICHES

½ cup butter, melted
2 Tbsp. prepared mustard
1 Tbsp. dried minced onion
1 Tbsp. poppy seeds
2 to 3 tsp. sugar
8 hamburger buns, split
8 slices Colby cheese
16 thin slices deli ham
   (about 1 lb.)
1½ cups shredded part-skim
   mozzarella cheese

1. In a small bowl, combine the butter, mustard, onion, poppy seeds and sugar. Place the bun bottoms, cut side up, in an ungreased 15x10x1-in. baking pan. Top each with Colby cheese, ham and mozzarella. Brush with half of the butter mixture.

2. Replace bun tops. Brush with remaining butter mixture. Bake, uncovered, at 350° until cheese is melted, 10-15 minutes.

1 SANDWICH: 504 cal., 32g fat (18g sat. fat), 102mg chol., 1444mg sod., 27g carb. (5g sugars, 1g fiber), 27g pro.

KITCHEN TIP: Feel free to substitute your favorite cheeses into this recipe. For instance, swap Colby with cheddar.

KANSAS CUCUMBER SALAD

Cucumbers are my favorite garden vegetable, so I use this recipe often.
It keeps very well in the refrigerator—that is, if you have any left.

—*Karen Ann Bland, Gove, KS*

PREP: 10 MIN. + CHILLING • **MAKES:** 8 SERVINGS

1 cup Miracle Whip
¼ cup sugar
4 tsp. cider vinegar
½ tsp. dill weed
½ tsp. salt, optional
4 medium cucumbers,
   peeled and thinly sliced
3 green onions, chopped

In a large bowl, combine Miracle Whip, sugar, vinegar, dill and, if desired, salt; mix well. Add cucumbers and onions; toss. Cover and chill for at least 1 hour.

⅔ CUP: 122 cal., 7g fat (1g sat. fat), 2mg chol., 201mg sod., 12g carb. (10g sugars, 2g fiber), 2g pro.

MEAT LOAF PIZZA CUPS

Fix and freeze these moist little meat loaves packed with pizza flavor. Try reheating for lunch, a snack or even a quick dinner. My family likes to drizzle extra pizza sauce on top.

—*Susan Wollin, Marshall, WI*

TAKES: 30 MIN. • MAKES: 1 DOZEN

 1 **large egg, lightly beaten**
 ½ **cup pizza sauce**
 ¼ **cup seasoned**
     bread crumbs
 ½ **tsp. Italian seasoning**
1½ **lbs. ground beef**
1½ **cups shredded part-skim**
     mozzarella cheese
     Optional: Additional pizza
     sauce and basil leaves

1. Preheat oven to 375°. In a large bowl, mix first 4 ingredients. Add beef; mix lightly but thoroughly. Divide into 12 portions; press each onto the bottom and up sides of a greased muffin cup. Add cheese to centers.

2. Bake until meat is cooked through, 15-18 minutes. If desired, top with additional sauce and basil before serving.

FREEZE OPTION: Freeze cooled meat loaves in freezer containers. To use, partially thaw in the refrigerator overnight. Microwave, covered, on high in a microwave-safe dish until heated through.

2 MEAT LOAF CUPS: 327 cal., 20g fat (8g sat. fat), 119mg chol., 416mg sod., 6g carb. (2g sugars, 1g fiber), 29g pro.

CLOCKWISE FROM RIGHT:

FUTURE FARMER
"Justine learned about farm life the right way, from her cowboy grandpa."

—*DarAnn Curry, Belgrade, Montana*

SCENIC ROUTE
"This corncrib is tucked away on an old homeplace not far from where I live. I pass it every day, and I had to stop and take a picture of this gorgeous scene."

—*Donna Johnson, Woodlawn, Virginia*

LUNCHTIME
"My daughter, Alexis, is smitten with kittens in this photo. Alexis might be only 2 here, but she has a caring parental look as she cuddles cute Blacky The Kitten at kitty feeding time."

—*Tanya Hanson, Amery, Wisconsin*

TABLE FOR ONE
"Snowcap lives on a local farm, and I'm sure he was happy to have a pasture full grass and dandelions to munch on for lunch."
—*Carolyn Anderson,*
New Alexandria, Pennsylvania

TURKEY & APPLE ARUGULA SALAD

We eat turkey all the time—not just at the holidays. You'll enjoy its flavor
year-round in this quick yet refreshing salad with fresh fruit and salad greens.

—Nancy Heishman, Las Vegas, NV

TAKES: 20 MIN. • MAKES: 6 SERVINGS

½ cup orange juice
3 Tbsp. red wine vinegar
3 Tbsp. sesame oil
2 Tbsp. minced
  fresh chives
¼ tsp. salt
¼ tsp. coarsely
  ground pepper

SALAD
4 cups cubed cooked turkey
4 tsp. curry powder
½ tsp. freshly
  ground pepper
¼ tsp. salt
1 large apple, chopped
1 cup green grapes, halved
3 cups fresh arugula
  or baby spinach
1 can (11 oz.) mandarin
  oranges, drained
½ cup chopped walnuts
½ cup pomegranate seeds

1. For dressing, whisk together first 6 ingredients.

2. Place turkey in a large bowl; sprinkle with seasonings and
toss to combine. Stir in the apple and grapes. Add arugula
and mandarin oranges. Drizzle with the dressing; toss lightly
to combine.

3. Sprinkle with chopped walnuts and pomegranate seeds.
Serve immediately.

1½ CUPS: 354 cal., 17g fat (3g sat. fat), 94mg chol., 301mg sod., 22g
carb. (17g sugars, 3g fiber), 30g pro.

41

FIREHOUSE CHILI

As one of the cooks at our firehouse, I used to prepare meals for 10 men. This hearty chili was always one of their favorites.
—*Richard Clements, San Dimas, CA*

PREP: 20 MIN. • COOK: 1½ HOURS • MAKES: 16 SERVINGS (4 QT.)

2 Tbsp. canola oil
4 lbs. lean ground beef (90% lean)
2 medium onions, chopped
1 medium green pepper, chopped
4 cans (16 oz. each) kidney beans, rinsed and drained
3 cans (28 oz. each) stewed tomatoes, cut up
1 can (14½ oz.) beef broth
3 Tbsp. chili powder
2 Tbsp. ground coriander
2 Tbsp. ground cumin
4 garlic cloves, minced
1 tsp. dried oregano

In a Dutch oven, heat canola oil over medium heat. Brown beef in batches, crumbling meat, until no longer pink; drain and set aside. Add onions and green pepper; cook until tender. Return meat to Dutch oven. Stir in remaining ingredients. Bring to a boil. Reduce heat; simmer, covered, until flavors are blended, about 1½ hours.

1 CUP: 354 cal., 12g fat (4g sat. fat), 71mg chol., 657mg sod., 32g carb. (10g sugars, 8g fiber), 31g pro.

DIABETIC EXCHANGES: 3 lean meat, 2 starch.

KITCHEN TIP: Canola oil is high in monounsaturated fat, a type that helps to decrease blood cholesterol levels, and low in saturated fat, which can increase blood cholesterol. Olive oil would also taste great in this chili recipe and has the same healthy-fat properties.

CHICKEN, NECTARINE & AVOCADO SALAD

This salad is so refreshing, and it comes together very quickly. Using a nutty granola adds crunch and makes it different. It's not the time for chocolate granola, though!

—*Elisabeth Larsen, Pleasant Grove, UT*

TAKES: 15 MIN. • MAKES: 4 SERVINGS

6 oz. fresh baby spinach
(about 8 cups)
2 medium nectarines,
thinly sliced
2 cups cubed cooked
chicken
1 cup crumbled feta cheese
½ cup poppy seed
salad dressing
1 medium ripe avocado,
peeled and sliced
1 cup granola with
fruit and nuts

In a large bowl, combine spinach, nectarines, chicken and feta. Drizzle with dressing; toss to coat. Top with avocado slices and granola. Serve immediately.

1½ CUPS: 561 cal., 32g fat (7g sat. fat), 87mg chol., 539mg sod., 38g carb. (18g sugars, 7g fiber), 30g pro.

KITCHEN TIP: Try this easy dish with leftover rotisserie chicken, or grill up a few extra chicken breasts during your next barbecue. The flame-broiled poultry is wonderful in this recipe.

IT WAS A POTATO SOUP WINTER

BY TERESA AMBORD ANDERSON, CALIFORNIA

There was a common question in our house one winter. "Potato soup again?" my sisters and I asked almost in unison as we walked through the door after school. But it wasn't a complaint—we loved potato soup. We were just puzzled about why we were lucky enough to have it so often.

"Yep," answered our stepmom, Polly. "Girls, put your books away and then come and tell me how school was while you set the table." As I passed the stove, I peeked in the soup pot and breathed in the wonderful aroma. "I hope you made enough so we can have leftovers!" I said. I didn't always love the meals Polly fixed—not because she wasn't a good cook, but because I was a moody teenager and a picky eater.

But her potato soup was creamy, oniony and perfectly seasoned. Until that winter, our first living as "country folk," she'd only made it once in a while. Then, out of the blue, we were having it a few times every week, and we girls couldn't believe our good fortune.

By the time we'd set the table and told Polly about school, Dad arrived home. Polly put bowls of hot potato soup in front of us. Accompanied by salad and homemade bread, and orange slices for dessert, this dinner never disappointed.

After dinner, my little sisters cleared the table and I washed the dishes. As usual, Dad and Polly retreated to the living room to talk about the day. I could hear Dad talk about work at the mill. Then they grew quieter, leaned toward each other and talked in hushed tones. I was a self-absorbed teen, so I noticed, but only slightly.

I thought about the day 6 months earlier, when we'd left our home in Southern California and moved 700 miles north to rural California.

I was angry about the move, and to make it all worse, we didn't move into a house. Instead, we camped in a tent all summer while Dad built a cabin. The process was fraught with problems, including a delay after Dad broke his leg.

When we moved into the cabin that fall, a neighbor brought us an unusual gift. It was a giant burlap sack of russet potatoes, a locally grown crop. Our neighbor probably had no idea how important that gift would become.

The bag contained so many potatoes we had them fried, baked, mashed—you name it, we ate it. Fortunately, Dad had dug a root cellar to keep those potatoes fresh longer.

Our parents never discussed money problems with us. They never let on that the nest egg we'd been living on had been depleted, mostly due to unexpected doctor bills from Dad's broken leg and the construction delay. So even after Dad started back to work, it took time for all of the money issues to smooth out.

Courtesy of our thoughtful new neighbor, our potato soup winter helped keep us well-fed despite my parents' worries. Unsuspecting, we happily feasted on spuds all winter long.

Years later, when my sisters and I had our own families, we finally put the pieces together. We hadn't really hit the dinner jackpot; Polly was working with a limited budget, and meat was certainly just out of the question sometimes.

I'd had such a bad attitude about moving to the country, but I came to realize it was the best decision my parents could have made. From the slower-paced life to the new dear friends who gave us that beautiful bag of spuds, there were many unexpected blessings to be had. That winter, the frequent meals of potato soup showed us how tough our parents were, and proved to me how truly great the country life is.

See Polly's Perfect Potato Soup recipe on page 48.

POLLY'S PERFECT POTATO SOUP

When we lived in rural California, my stepmom, Polly, made this heartwarming soup.
Served with loaves of homemade bread and a fresh green salad, it was always a hit.

—Teresa Ambord, Anderson, CA

PREP TIME: 15 MIN. COOK TIME: 30 MIN. • MAKES: 8 SERVINGS (2½ QT.)

6   medium potatoes, (about
    4 lbs.) peeled and cubed
3   cups whole milk
½   cup heavy whipping
    cream
2   Tbsp. unsalted butter
1   garlic clove, minced
1¼ tsp. kosher salt
1   tsp. coarsely
    ground pepper
½   tsp. seasoned salt
6   green onions,
    thinly sliced
    Optional: Shredded
    cheddar cheese and
    crumbled bacon

1. Place potatoes In a large stockpot or Dutch oven; cover with cold water. Bring to a boil. Cook, uncovered until very tender, 20-25 minutes; drain well, reserving 1 cup liquid.

2. Return potatoes to stockpot or Dutch oven; mash until desired consistency. Return pan to heat and add milk, heavy cream, butter, garlic and seasonings; heat on medium-low until heated through, 5-10 minutes, adding reserved cooking liquid to thin soup to desired consistency. Serve warm. Top with green onions. If desired, sprinkle with cheese and bacon.

1¼ CUPS: 230 cal., 11g fat (7g sat. fat), 34mg chol., 444mg sod., 28g carb. (7g sugars, 2g fiber), 6g pro.

GRILLED FIRECRACKER POTATO SALAD

I could eat potato salad all the time. A little spice is nice, so I use cayenne
and paprika in this side dish that comes with its own fireworks.
—*Ashley Armstrong, Kingsland, GA*

PREP: 20 MIN. • GRILL: 20 MIN. + CHILLING • MAKES: 16 SERVINGS

- 3 lbs. small red potatoes (about 30), quartered
- 2 Tbsp. olive oil
- 1 tsp. salt
- ½ tsp. pepper

DRESSING
- 1½ cups mayonnaise
- ½ cup finely chopped onion
- ¼ cup Dijon mustard
- 2 Tbsp. sweet pickle relish
- ½ tsp. paprika
- ¼ tsp. cayenne pepper

SALAD
- 6 hard-boiled large eggs, chopped
- 2 celery ribs, finely chopped
  Minced fresh chives, optional

1. Toss potatoes with oil, salt and pepper; place in a grill wok or basket. Grill, covered, over medium heat 20-25 minutes or until potatoes are tender, stirring occasionally. Transfer potatoes to a large bowl; cool slightly.

2. In a small bowl, mix dressing ingredients. Add dressing, eggs and celery to potatoes; toss to combine. Refrigerate, covered, 1-2 hours or until cold. If desired, sprinkle with chives.

1 CUP: 265 cal., 20g fat (3g sat. fat), 77mg chol., 398mg sod., 16g carb. (2g sugars, 2g fiber), 4g pro.

KITCHEN TIP: If you do not have a grill wok or basket, use a large disposable foil pan and poke holes in the bottom of the pan.

BLUE RIBBON WINNER

SPICY BUFFALO CHICKEN WRAPS

This recipe has a real kick and is one of my husband's favorites. It's ready in a flash, is easily doubled and is the closest thing to restaurant Buffalo wings I've ever tasted—but lighter!

—Jennifer Beck, Meridian, ID

TAKES: 25 MIN. • MAKES: 2 SERVINGS

½ lb. boneless skinless chicken breast, cubed
½ tsp. canola oil
2 Tbsp. Louisiana-style hot sauce
1 cup shredded lettuce
2 flour tortillas (6 in.), warmed
2 tsp. reduced-fat ranch salad dressing
2 Tbsp. crumbled blue cheese

1. In a large nonstick skillet, cook chicken in oil over medium heat for 6 minutes; drain. Stir in hot sauce. Bring to a boil. Reduce heat; simmer, uncovered, until sauce is thickened and chicken is no longer pink, 3-5 minutes.

2. Place lettuce on tortillas; drizzle with ranch dressing. Top with chicken mixture and blue cheese; roll up.

1 WRAP: 273 cal., 11g fat (3g sat. fat), 70mg chol., 453mg sod., 15g carb. (1g sugars, 1g fiber), 28g pro.

DIABETIC EXCHANGES: 3 lean meat, 1½ fat, 1 starch.

LEMONY TURKEY RICE SOUP

While growing up in Texas, I spent a lot of time helping my grandma cook.
Lemon and cilantro add a deliciously different twist to this turkey soup.

—*Margarita Cuellar, East Chicago, IN*

TAKES: 30 MIN. • MAKES: 8 SERVINGS (2 QT.)

2 cups diced cooked turkey
2 cups cooked long
   grain rice
1 can (10¾ oz.) condensed
   cream of chicken
   soup, undiluted
¼ tsp. pepper
6 cups chicken
   broth, divided
2 Tbsp. cornstarch
¼ to ⅓ cup lemon juice
¼ to ½ cup minced
   fresh cilantro

1. In a large saucepan, combine first 4 ingredients and 5½ cups broth. Bring to a boil; cook 3 minutes.

2. In a small bowl, mix cornstarch and remaining broth until smooth; gradually stir into soup. Bring to a boil; cook and stir until thickened, 1-2 minutes. Remove from heat; stir in lemon juice and cilantro.

1 CUP: 166 cal., 4g fat (1g sat. fat), 42mg chol., 1047mg sod., 17g carb. (1g sugars, 1g fiber), 13g pro.

BACON-BLUE CHEESE STUFFED BURGERS

These loaded burgers make a great lunch or dinner. They're sure to satisfy all of the big appetites at your table. Add some potato chips and call everyone to lunch!

—*Christine Keating, Norwalk, CA*

PREP: 30 MIN. • GRILL: 10 MIN. • MAKES: 4 BURGERS

1½ lbs. lean ground beef (90% lean)
3 oz. cream cheese, softened
⅓ cup crumbled blue cheese
⅓ cup bacon bits
½ tsp. salt
½ tsp. garlic powder
¼ tsp. pepper
1 lb. sliced fresh mushrooms
1 Tbsp. olive oil
1 Tbsp. water
1 Tbsp. Dijon mustard
4 whole wheat hamburger buns, split
¼ cup mayonnaise
4 romaine leaves
1 medium tomato, sliced

1. Shape beef into 8 thin patties. Combine the cream cheese, blue cheese and bacon bits; spoon onto the center of 4 patties. Top with remaining patties and press edges firmly to seal. Combine the salt, garlic powder and pepper; sprinkle over the patties.

2. Grill burgers, covered, over medium heat or broil 4 in. from the heat on each side until a thermometer reads 160° and juices run clear, 5-7 minutes.

3. Meanwhile, in a large skillet, saute mushrooms in oil until tender. Stir in water and mustard.

4. Serve burgers on buns with mayonnaise, romaine, tomato and mushroom mixture.

1 BURGER: 701 cal., 43g fat (15g sat. fat), 149mg chol., 1280mg sod., 31g carb. (7g sugars, 5g fiber), 48g pro.

HERB & CHEESE-STUFFED BURGERS: Omit blue cheese and bacon bits. Mix cream cheese with ¼ cup shredded cheddar cheese, 2 Tbsp. minced fresh parsley and 1 tsp. Dijon mustard. Season meat with ¾ tsp. crushed dried rosemary and ¼ dried sage leaves. Proceed as recipe directs.

GREEK-STUFFED BURGERS: Omit cream cheese, blue cheese and bacon bits. Mix ⅓ cup feta cheese, ⅓ cup chopped tomato, 2 Tbsp. chopped red onion, 4 tsp. chopped ripe olives, 2 tsp. olive oil and ¼ tsp. dried oregano. Stuff burgers with feta mixture and proceed as recipe directs.

BLUE
RIBBON
WINNER

CHERRY TOMATO SALAD

This recipe evolved from a need to use the bumper crops of cherry tomatoes we grow. It's become a summer-favorite salad at our house.
—*Sally Sibley, St. Augustine, FL*

PREP: 15 MIN. + MARINATING • MAKES: 6 SERVINGS

1 qt. cherry tomatoes, halved
¼ cup canola oil
3 Tbsp. white vinegar
½ tsp. salt
½ tsp. sugar
¼ cup minced fresh parsley
1 to 2 tsp. minced fresh basil
1 to 2 tsp. minced fresh oregano

Place tomatoes in a shallow bowl. In a small bowl, whisk oil, vinegar, salt and sugar until blended; stir in herbs. Pour over tomatoes; gently toss to coat. Refrigerate, covered, overnight.

¾ CUP: 103 cal., 10g fat (1g sat. fat), 0 chol., 203mg sod., 4g carb. (3g sugars, 1g fiber), 1g pro.

DIABETIC EXCHANGES: 2 fat, 1 vegetable.

LITTLE HELPER
"Gathering eggs is my daughter's favorite chore on the farm. Cora is a compassionate, happy country girl."
—*Sara Rogers,*
Coxs Creek, Kentucky

FROM TOP:

PEAS IN A POD
"This runt piglet and adorable puppy became fast friends."
—*Cathy Cooper, Covington, Indiana*

CUTE COWHAND
"Baylor, my 2-year-old son, is the sixth-generation farmer on our family ranch."
—*Shelby Hill, Tonto Basin, Arizona*

WHITE CHILI WITH A KICK

Store-bought rotisserie chicken makes this spicy chili easy, but you could also cook your own if you prefer. We like to top our bowls with sour cream, green onions, cheese or salsa.
—*Emmajean Anderson, Mendota Heights, MN*

PREP: 20 MIN. • COOK: 15 MIN. • MAKES: 9 SERVINGS (2¼ QT.)

1 large onion, chopped
6 Tbsp. butter, cubed
2 Tbsp. all-purpose flour
2 cups chicken broth
¾ cup half-and-half cream
1 rotisserie chicken, cut up
2 cans (15 oz. each) cannellini beans, rinsed and drained
1 can (11 oz.) white corn, drained
2 cans (4 oz. each) chopped green chiles
2 tsp. ground cumin
1 tsp. chili powder
½ tsp. salt
½ tsp. white pepper
½ tsp. hot pepper sauce
1½ cups shredded pepper jack cheese
   Optional: Salsa and chopped green onions

1. In a Dutch oven, saute the onion in butter. Stir in flour until blended; cook and stir until golden brown, about 3 minutes. Gradually add broth and cream. Bring to a boil; cook and stir until thickened, about 2 minutes.

2. Add the chicken, beans, corn, chiles, cumin, chili powder, salt, pepper and pepper sauce; heat through. Gently stir in cheese until melted.

3. If desired, garnish each serving with salsa and green onions.

1 CUP: 424 cal., 21g fat (11g sat. fat), 113mg chol., 896mg sod., 26g carb. (3g sugars, 5g fiber), 31g pro.

FARMERS MARKET ORZO SALAD

Here, I use orzo as a base for grilled veggies in an easy lemony vinaigrette.
I add mozzarella, but it's also great with feta or smoked Gouda.

—Heather Dezzutto, Raleigh, NC

PREP: 25 MIN. • GRILL: 10 MIN. • MAKES: 8 SERVINGS

1 pkg. (16 oz.) orzo pasta
2 small yellow summer squash, halved lengthwise
1 medium zucchini, halved lengthwise
1 medium red onion, quartered
8 Tbsp. olive oil, divided
½ tsp. salt, divided
¼ tsp. pepper, divided
3 Tbsp. lemon juice
8 oz. smoked mozzarella cheese, cut into ¼-in. cubes
1½ cups grape tomatoes, halved lengthwise
½ cup chopped fresh basil
½ cup pine nuts, toasted

1. Cook the orzo according to package directions; drain. Brush yellow squash, zucchini and onion with 2 Tbsp. oil; sprinkle with ¼ tsp. salt and ⅛ tsp. pepper. Grill the vegetables, covered, over medium heat or broil 4 in. from heat 10-12 minutes or until lightly charred and tender, turning once. Cool slightly. Cut into 1-in. pieces.

2. In a small bowl, whisk lemon juice and remaining oil until blended. In a large bowl, combine orzo, grilled vegetables, mozzarella, tomatoes, basil and remaining salt and pepper. Add dressing; toss to coat. Sprinkle with pine nuts.

1¼ CUPS: 291 cal., 27g fat (7g sat. fat), 25mg chol., 274mg sod., 7g carb. (4g sugars, 2g fiber), 9g pro.

TOMATO, AVOCADO & GRILLED CORN SALAD

With ripe tomatoes, fresh basil and grilled corn, this sunny salad tastes just like summertime!
Enjoy it on its own for lunch or add it to dinner as a side. Either way, it's lovely.

—Angela Spengler, Niceville, FL

PREP: 20 MIN. • GRILL: 10 MIN. + COOLING • MAKES: 8 SERVINGS

1 medium ear sweet
   corn, husks removed
3 large red tomatoes,
   sliced
3 large yellow
   tomatoes, sliced
¾ tsp. kosher salt, divided
½ tsp. pepper, divided
2 medium ripe avocados,
   peeled and sliced
¼ cup olive oil
2 Tbsp. red wine vinegar
1 Tbsp. minced fresh basil,
   plus more for garnish
⅓ cup crumbled feta cheese

1. Grill corn, covered, over medium heat 10-12 minutes or until lightly browned and tender, turning occasionally. Cool slightly. Cut corn from cob.

2. Arrange tomato slices on a large serving platter. Sprinkle with ½ tsp. salt and ¼ tsp. pepper. Top with avocado slices. Whisk together the oil, vinegar, basil and remaining salt and pepper; drizzle half over the tomatoes and avocado. Top with grilled corn and feta; drizzle remaining dressing over top. Garnish with additional chopped basil.

1 SERVING: 164 cal., 13g fat (2g sat. fat), 3mg chol., 237mg sod., 11g carb. (4g sugars, 4g fiber), 3g pro.

DIABETIC EXCHANGES: 2 fat, 1 vegetable, ½ starch.

KITCHEN TIP: This dish is spectacular with fresh heirloom tomatoes, and a great way to use up a bumper crop. Best of all, the amped-up flavor means you can cut back on the salt. For a quick, healthy dinner, top with grilled chicken.

TANGY PULLED PORK SANDWICHES

Set the slow cooker early in the morning, and these tender, moist sandwiches will be ready for lunch. They're so comforting, you'll come to rely on the recipe.
—*Beki Kosydar-Krantz, Mayfield, PA*

PREP: 10 MIN. • **COOK:** 4 HOURS • **MAKES:** 4 SERVINGS

1 pork tenderloin (1 lb.)
1 cup ketchup
2 Tbsp. plus 1½ tsp. brown sugar
2 Tbsp. plus 1½ tsp. cider vinegar
1 Tbsp. plus 1½ tsp. Worcestershire sauce
1 Tbsp. spicy brown mustard
¼ tsp. pepper
4 rolls or buns, split and toasted

1. Cut the tenderloin in half; place in a 3-qt. slow cooker. Combine the ketchup, brown sugar, vinegar, Worcestershire sauce, mustard and pepper; pour over pork.

2. Cover and cook on low for 4-5 hours or until meat is tender. Remove the meat; shred with 2 forks. Return to the slow cooker; heat through. Serve on toasted rolls or buns.

1 SANDWICH: 402 cal., 7g fat (2g sat. fat), 63mg chol., 1181mg sod., 56g carb. (18g sugars, 2g fiber), 29g pro.

CHAPTER 3
OVEN-FRESH BREADS & MORE

Take a deep breath and relish the heavenly aroma of freshly baked bread. Buttery biscuits, golden rolls, sweet surprises and other specialties make every house a home.

NO-KNEAD KNOT ROLLS

My mom, Velma Perkins, loved to serve these light, golden rolls when I was growing up on our Iowa farm. They're extra nice since they require no kneading.
—*Toni Hilscher, Omaha, NE*

PREP: 25 MIN. + RISING • **BAKE:** 10 MIN. • **MAKES:** 4 DOZEN

2 pkg. (¼ oz. each) active dry yeast
2 cups warm water (110° to 115°)
½ cup sugar
2 tsp. salt
6 to 6½ cups all-purpose flour
1 large egg, room temperature
½ cup shortening
½ cup butter, softened

1. In a large bowl, dissolve yeast in warm water. Add the sugar, salt and 2 cups flour. Beat on medium speed for 2 minutes. Beat in egg and shortening. Stir in enough remaining flour to form a soft dough (do not knead). Cover and refrigerate overnight.

2. Punch the dough down and divide into 4 portions; roll each portion into a 14x12-in. rectangle. Spread 2 Tbsp. butter over dough. Fold in half lengthwise; cut into 12 strips. Tie each strip into a knot; tuck and pinch ends under. Place 2 in. apart on greased baking sheets. Repeat with remaining dough.

3. Cover and let rise until doubled, about 1 hour. Bake at 400° until golden brown, 10-12 minutes. Remove to wire rack to cool.

1 ROLL: 102 cal., 4g fat (2g sat. fat), 10mg chol., 119mg sod., 14g carb. (2g sugars, 0 fiber), 2g pro.

CINNAMON SWIRL BREAD

Your family will be impressed with the soft texture and appealing swirls of cinnamon in these lovely loaves. Slices are delightful any time of day.

—Diane Armstrong, Elm Grove, WI

PREP: 25 MIN. + RISING • BAKE: 30 MIN. • MAKES: 2 LOAVES (16 SLICES EACH)

2 pkg. (¼ oz. each) active dry yeast
⅓ cup warm water (110° to 115°)
1 cup warm whole milk (110° to 115°)
1 cup sugar, divided
2 large eggs, room temperature
6 Tbsp. butter, softened
1½ tsp. salt
5½ to 6 cups all-purpose flour
2 Tbsp. ground cinnamon

1. In a large bowl, dissolve the yeast in warm water. Add milk, ½ cup sugar, eggs, butter, salt and 3 cups flour; beat on medium speed until smooth. Stir in enough remaining flour to form a soft dough.

2. Turn dough onto a floured surface; knead until smooth and elastic, 6-8 minutes. Place in a greased bowl, turning once to grease the top. Cover; let rise in a warm place until doubled, about 1 hour.

3. Mix cinnamon and remaining sugar. Punch down dough. Turn onto a lightly floured surface; divide in half. Roll each portion into an 18x8-in. rectangle; sprinkle each with about ¼ cup cinnamon sugar to within ½ in. of edges. Roll up jelly-roll style, starting with a short side; pinch seam to seal. Place in 2 greased 9x5-in. loaf pans, seam side down.

4. Cover with kitchen towels; let rise in a warm place until doubled, about 1½ hours. Preheat oven to 350°.

5. Bake until golden brown, 30-35 minutes. Remove from pans to wire racks to cool.

1 SLICE: 132 cal., 3g fat (2g sat. fat), 20mg chol., 141mg sod., 23g carb. (7g sugars, 1g fiber), 3g pro.

ROLLED BUTTERMILK BISCUITS

I scribbled down this recipe when our family visited The Farmers' Museum in Cooperstown, New York, more than 25 years ago. I must have gotten it right, because these biscuits turn out great every time.

—*Patricia Kile, Elizabethtown, PA*

PREP: 20 MIN. • BAKE: 15 MIN. • MAKES: 8 BISCUITS

2 cups all-purpose flour
3 tsp. baking powder
½ tsp. baking soda
¼ tsp. salt
3 Tbsp. cold butter
¾ to 1 cup buttermilk
1 Tbsp. fat-free milk

1. Preheat oven to 450°. In a large bowl, combine the flour, baking powder, baking soda and salt; cut in butter until mixture resembles coarse crumbs. Stir in enough buttermilk just to moisten dough.

2. Turn onto a lightly floured surface; knead 3-4 times. Pat or roll to ¾-in. thickness. Cut with a floured 2½-in. biscuit cutter. Place in a large ungreased cast-iron or other ovenproof skillet.

3. Brush with milk. Bake until golden brown, 12-15 minutes.

1 BISCUIT: 162 cal., 5g fat (3g sat. fat), 12mg chol., 412mg sod., 25g carb. (1g sugars, 1g fiber), 4g pro.

DIABETIC EXCHANGES: 1½ starch, 1 fat.

CELERY-ONION POPOVERS

I found this handwritten recipe in a cookbook I received from my mom. Featuring onion and celery, these pleasing popovers taste a little bit like Thanksgiving stuffing.

—*Barbara Carlucci, Orange Park, FL*

PREP: 15 MIN. • BAKE: 40 MIN. • MAKES: 9 POPOVERS

2 cups all-purpose flour
1 tsp. onion salt
⅛ tsp. celery salt
4 large eggs, room temperature
2 cups whole milk
¼ cup grated onion
¼ cup grated celery
3 Tbsp. butter, melted

1. In a large bowl, combine the flour, onion salt and celery salt. Combine the eggs, milk, onion, celery and butter; whisk into the dry ingredients just until blended. Grease and flour the bottom and sides of 9 popover cups; fill two-thirds full with batter.

2. Bake at 450° for 15 minutes. Reduce heat to 350° (do not open oven door). Bake 25 minutes longer or until deep golden brown (do not underbake). Immediately cut a slit in the top of each popover to allow steam to escape.

1 POPOVER: 202 cal., 8g fat (4g sat. fat), 98mg chol., 306mg sod., 25g carb. (3g sugars, 1g fiber), 7g pro.

THE SWEET LIFE

TOPASHAW FARMS VARDAMAN, MISSISSIPPI

Nearly 40 years ago, the husband-and-wife team of Joe and Melissa Edmondson decided to focus their energies on sweet potatoes. It's a crop with deep roots in the South and an enduring presence on southern menus.

"For Thanksgiving, you just have to have sweet potatoes on the table," Melissa says. "Sweet potato pie, sweet potato casserole..."

Melissa and Joe both grew up on farms, later venturing out on their own with 125 acres in Vardaman, Mississippi. Over time, they expanded the farm, named after nearby Topashaw Creek, to 3,000 acres of rotating cropland.

They also grow cotton and raise cattle. But by specializing in sweet potatoes, they have become experts on the shape, size and skin quality of this beloved tuber. In addition, they've mastered the techniques behind testing new varieties and conditioning the soil to meet crop needs.

In 2009, after floods damaged 200 acres of cropland, Melissa and Joe decided to build storage and packing facilities. In doing so, they eliminated the middleman, gaining more control over their product and business. Plus, the facility allows them to buy sweet potatoes from other farmers and to ship product across the United States and into Canada year-round.

Melissa and Joe's kids, now grown, are carrying on the family business. "Farming has been good to us and our children," Melissa says.

From top: The harvest; Joe Edmondson stops for a photo; a few of Melissa and Joe's grandkids sit for a picture with farm employees; potato diggers get the job done.

SWEET POTATO SPICE BREAD

It's a good thing this recipe makes two mini loaves because they'll go fast!
For a small household, eat one loaf now and freeze the other for later.

—Ronnie Littles, Virginia Beach, VA

PREP: 15 MIN. • **BAKE:** 25 MIN. + COOLING • **MAKES:** 2 MINI LOAVES (6 SLICES EACH)

1 cup all-purpose flour
1½ tsp. baking powder
¼ tsp. each ground cinnamon, nutmeg and allspice
⅛ tsp. salt
1 large egg, room temperature
⅓ cup mashed sweet potato
⅓ cup honey
3 Tbsp. canola oil
2 Tbsp. molasses
⅓ cup chopped walnuts

1. In a small bowl, combine the flour, baking powder, spices and salt. In another small bowl, whisk the egg, sweet potato, honey, oil and molasses. Stir into dry ingredients just until moistened. Fold in walnuts.

2. Transfer to two 5¾x3x2-in. loaf pans coated with cooking spray. Bake at 325° for 25-30 minutes or until a toothpick inserted in the center comes out clean. Cool for 10 minutes before removing from pans to wire racks.

1 SLICE: 142 cal., 6g fat (1g sat. fat), 18mg chol., 85mg sod., 20g carb. (10g sugars, 1g fiber), 3g pro.

DIABETIC EXCHANGES: 1½ starch, 1 fat.

BLUE RIBBON WINNER

CHIVE PINWHEEL ROLLS

These light, pleasant-tasting dinner rolls complement almost any entree. With the chive filling swirled through a golden bread, they're suited for weeknight meals and special occasions alike.

—*Ann Niemela, Ely, MN*

PREP: 25 MIN. + RISING • BAKE: 30 MIN. • MAKES: 15 ROLLS

3½ cups all-purpose flour
3 Tbsp. sugar
1 pkg. (¼ oz.) active
   dry yeast
1½ tsp. salt
1 cup 2% milk
⅓ cup canola oil
¼ cup water
¼ cup mashed potatoes
   (without added
   milk and butter)
1 large egg, room
   temperature

CHIVE FILLING
1 cup sour cream
1 cup minced chives
1 large egg yolk
   Butter, melted

1. In a large bowl, combine 2½ cups flour, sugar, yeast and salt. In a small saucepan, heat milk, oil, water and mashed potatoes to 120°-130°. Add to dry ingredients; beat just until moistened. Add egg; beat until smooth. Stir in enough remaining flour to form a soft dough.

2. Turn onto a floured surface; knead until smooth and elastic, 6-8 minutes. Place in a greased bowl; turn once to grease top. Cover and let rise in a warm place until doubled, about 1 hour.

3. Turn dough onto a floured surface. Roll into a 15x10-in. rectangle. In a bowl, combine sour cream, chives and egg yolk. Spread over dough to within ½ in. of edges.

4. Roll up jelly-roll style, starting with a long side; pinch seam to seal. Cut into 1-in. slices. Place cut side down in a 13x9-in. baking pan. Cover and let rise until doubled, about 1 hour.

5. Bake at 350° for 30-35 minutes or until golden brown. Brush with butter. Cool on a wire rack. Refrigerate leftovers.

1 ROLL: 214 cal., 9g fat (3g sat. fat), 41mg chol., 258mg sod., 27g carb. (4g sugars, 1g fiber), 5g pro.

BUTTERY BUBBLE BREAD

This fun-to-eat monkey bread, baked in a fluted tube pan, is easy and almost foolproof.
If I'm serving it for breakfast, I add some cinnamon and drizzle it with icing.

—*Pat Stevens, Granbury, TX*

PREP: 25 MIN. + RISING • BAKE: 30 MIN. • MAKES: 16 SERVINGS

1 pkg. (¼ oz.) active
   dry yeast
1 cup warm water
   (110° to 115°)
½ cup sugar
½ cup shortening
1 large egg, room
   temperature
½ tsp. salt
4 to 4½ cups all-purpose
   flour, divided
6 Tbsp. butter, melted

1. In a large bowl, dissolve yeast in warm water. Add the sugar, shortening, egg, salt and 1 cup of flour. Beat until smooth. Stir in enough remaining flour to form a soft dough.

2. Turn onto a floured surface; knead until smooth and elastic, 6-8 minutes. Place in a greased bowl, turning once to grease top. Cover and let rise in a warm place until doubled, about 1 hour.

3. Punch dough down. Turn onto a lightly floured surface; shape into 1½-in. balls. Dip the balls in butter and arrange evenly in a greased 9-in. fluted tube pan. Drizzle with remaining butter. Cover pan and let dough rise in a warm place until doubled, about 45 minutes.

4. Bake at 350° for 30-35 minutes or until golden brown. Cool for 5 minutes before inverting onto a serving platter. Serve bread warm.

1 SERVING: 237 cal., 11g fat (4g sat. fat), 25mg chol., 122mg sod., 30g carb. (7g sugars, 1g fiber), 4g pro.

KITCHEN TIP: Switch things up by adding chopped fresh herbs to the melted butter. Try a ½ tsp. each of minced thyme, rosemary and parsley.

SKILLET HERB CORNBREAD

My grandmother, aunts and mom were all good bakers, and each had a specialty when it came to bread. Mom's was my favorite! The flavors call to mind the taste of cornbread stuffing.

—*Shirley Smith, Yorba Linda, CA*

PREP: 10 MIN. • BAKE: 35 MIN. • MAKES: 10 SERVINGS

1½ cups all-purpose flour
2 Tbsp. sugar
4 tsp. baking powder
1½ tsp. salt
1 tsp. rubbed sage
1 tsp. dried thyme
1½ cups yellow cornmeal
1½ cups chopped celery
1 cup chopped onion
1 jar (2 oz.) chopped pimientos, drained
3 large eggs, room temperature, beaten
1½ cups fat-free milk
⅓ cup vegetable oil

In a large bowl, combine flour, sugar, baking powder, salt, sage and thyme. Combine cornmeal, celery, onion and pimientos; add to dry ingredients and mix well. Add eggs, milk and oil; stir just until moistened. Pour into a greased 10- or 11-in. ovenproof skillet. Bake at 400° for 35-45 minutes or until bread tests done. Serve warm.

1 SLICE: 275 cal., 9g fat (2g sat. fat), 57mg chol., 598mg sod., 40g carb. (6g sugars, 2g fiber), 7g pro.

BACON & SAGE BITES

These savory popovers are tastefully topped with crumbled bacon and fresh sage, making them a welcome change from traditional dinner rolls and biscuits.

—*Melissa Jelinek, Apple Valley, MN*

PREP: 15 MIN. • BAKE: 20 MIN. • MAKES: 1 DOZEN

5   bacon strips, chopped
2   Tbsp. butter, melted
1½ cups all-purpose flour
3   Tbsp. minced fresh
    sage, divided
½   tsp. salt
1½ cups 2% milk
3   large eggs, room
    temperature

1. In a large skillet, cook bacon over medium heat until crisp. Remove to paper towels with a slotted spoon; drain, reserving the drippings.

2. Transfer drippings to a measuring cup; add enough melted butter to measure ¼ cup. Pour into 12 ungreased muffin cups. Place in a 450° oven until hot.

3. Meanwhile, in a small bowl, combine the flour, 2 Tbsp. sage and salt; beat in milk and eggs until smooth. Fold in two-thirds of the bacon. Divide batter among prepared muffin cups.

4. Bake at 450° for 10 minutes. Reduce heat to 350° (do not open oven door). Bake 10-12 minutes longer or until puffed and golden brown. Sprinkle with remaining bacon and sage.

1 SERVING: 150 cal., 8g fat (3g sat. fat), 67mg chol., 224mg sod., 14g carb. (2g sugars, 0 fiber), 5g pro.

CLOCKWISE FROM RIGHT:

I GOT YOUR BACK
"Derby, a miniature donkey, lets Maxine hitch a ride on his back."

—*Richard Fischer, Calico Rock, Arkansas*

YOU GOT A FRIEND IN ME
"Samuel, the biggest little cowboy we know, gives his mare lots of 'scratchies'."

—*Hannah Strom, Lake Park, Minnesota*

HOWDY PARTNER
"My dear friend shows how ranchers used to grease windmills—by climbing up to the platform to do it by hand."

—*Beth Gibbons, Crawford, Nebraska*

HAPPY TO HELP
"It's hard to tell who is more excited to help feed the calves—my dog Rita or my grandson Evan."
—*Nancy Vandrie, Marion, Michigan*

SWEET ONION BREAD SKILLET

Because there are just a few ingredients in this recipe, you'll get the best results if you use the finest-quality foods, like a fresh Vidalia onion and aged Parmesan cheese.

—Lisa Speer, Palm Beach, FL

PREP: 25 MIN. • BAKE: 10 MIN. • MAKES: 4 SERVINGS

1 large sweet onion,
   thinly sliced
2 Tbsp. butter
2 Tbsp. olive oil, divided
1 can (13.8 oz.) refrigerated
   pizza crust
¼ cup grated Parmesan
   cheese

1. In a large cast-iron or other ovenproof skillet, saute onion in butter and 1 Tbsp. oil until softened. Reduce heat to medium-low; cook, stirring occasionally, 15-20 minutes or until golden brown. Set aside.

2. Brush bottom and sides of skillet with remaining oil. Unroll dough into skillet; flatten dough and build up edge slightly. Top with onion mixture and cheese. Bake at 450° until golden brown, 10-12 minutes. Cut into 4 wedges.

1 WEDGE: 415 cal., 17g fat (5g sat. fat), 19mg chol., 776mg sod., 53g carb. (9g sugars, 2g fiber), 11g pro.

DELICIOUS ALMOND BRAIDS

Similar to an almond crescent, this coffee cake is light and flaky with a rich
almond center. It's so versatile you can serve it for dessert, breakfast or brunch.
It tastes like it came from a high-end bakery, but puff pastry dough makes it easy.

—*Gina Idone, Staten Island, NY*

PREP: 25 MIN. • BAKE: 30 MIN. + COOLING • MAKES: 2 BRAIDS (6 SLICES EACH)

1 pkg. (7 oz.) almond paste
½ cup butter
½ cup sugar
1 large egg, room
    temperature
2 Tbsp. all-purpose flour
1 pkg. (17.3 oz.) frozen
    puff pastry, thawed

GLAZE
¾ cup plus 1 Tbsp.
    confectioners' sugar
2 Tbsp. 2% milk
½ tsp. almond extract
¼ cup sliced almonds,
    toasted

1. Preheat oven to 375°. Place the almond paste, butter and sugar in a food processor; cover and pulse until chopped. Add egg and flour; process until smooth.

2. Place puff pastry sheets onto a greased baking sheet. Spread half of the filling mixture down the center third of 1 pastry sheet. On each side, cut 8 strips about 3½ in. into the center. Starting at 1 end, fold alternating strips at an angle across filling. Pinch ends to seal. Repeat with the remaining pastry and filling.

3. Bake until golden brown, 30-35 minutes. Remove to a wire rack to cool completely.

4. Combine the confectioners' sugar, milk and almond extract. Drizzle over braids; sprinkle with sliced almonds. Cut into slices to serve.

1 SLICE: 430 cal., 25g fat (8g sat. fat), 38mg chol., 197mg sod., 49g carb. (22g sugars, 4g fiber), 6g pro.

CARDAMOM BRAID BREAD

I came across this recipe in 1983, and I have been making it regularly ever since.
It's a lovely, very traditional yeast bread that's perfect for gift giving.

—Rita Bergman, Olympia, WA

PREP: 30 MIN. + RISING • BAKE: 20 MIN. • MAKES: 2 LOAVES (20 SLICES EACH)

6 cups all-purpose flour
2 pkg. (¼ oz. each)
   active dry yeast
1½ tsp. ground cardamom
1 tsp. salt
1½ cups plus 2 Tbsp.
   whole milk, divided
½ cup butter, cubed
½ cup honey
2 large eggs, room
   temperature
2 Tbsp. sugar

1. In a large bowl, combine 2 cups flour, yeast, cardamom and salt. In a small saucepan, heat 1½ cups milk, butter and honey to 120°-130°. Add to dry ingredients; beat just until moistened. Add eggs; beat until smooth. Stir in enough remaining flour to form a firm dough (dough will be sticky).

2. Turn onto a floured surface; knead until smooth and elastic, 6-8 minutes. Place in a greased bowl, turning once to grease top. Cover and let rise in a warm place until doubled, about 45 minutes.

3. Punch dough down. Turn onto a lightly floured surface; divide in half. Divide each portion into thirds. Shape each into a 14-in. rope. Place 3 ropes on a greased baking sheet and braid; pinch ends to seal and tuck under. Repeat with remaining dough. Cover and let rise until doubled, about 30 minutes.

4. Brush with remaining milk and sprinkle with sugar. Bake at 375° for 20-25 minutes or until golden brown. Remove from pans to wire racks to cool.

1 SLICE: 114 cal., 3g fat (2g sat. fat), 18mg chol., 91mg sod., 19g carb. (5g sugars, 1g fiber), 3g pro.

CINNAMON APPLE CIDER MONKEY BREAD

Cinnamon and apple cider easily turn tubes of plain cinnamon rolls into
monkey bread. It's a hit with my boys, who love all of the sticky sweetness.

—Kelly Walsh, Aviston, IL

PREP: 20 MIN. • BAKE: 45 MIN. + STANDING • MAKES: 16 SERVINGS

5 envelopes (.74 oz. each)
   instant spiced cider mix
3 tubes (12.4 oz. each)
   refrigerated cinnamon
   rolls with icing
2 medium Granny
   Smith apples, peeled
   and chopped
1 cup chopped pecans
   or walnuts
6 Tbsp. butter, melted
2 tsp. ground cinnamon

1. Preheat oven to 350°. Combine cider mixes. Separate cinnamon rolls, setting aside icings; cut each roll into quarters. Add to cider mixture; toss to coat.

2. Arrange a third of the dough pieces in a well-greased 10-in. fluted tube pan; top with half of the apples and half of the pecans. Repeat layers once. Top with remaining dough.

3. Mix melted butter, cinnamon and icing from 1 container until blended. Drizzle over top of the rolls. Bake until golden brown, 45-50 minutes. (If needed, cover top loosely with foil during last 5 minutes to prevent overbrowning.)

4. Immediately invert monkey bread onto a serving plate; keep pan inverted 10 minutes, allowing bread to release. Remove pan. Meanwhile, microwave remaining icing, uncovered, until softened, about 10 seconds. Drizzle icing over monkey bread. Serve warm.

1 SERVING: 329 cal., 17g fat (5g sat. fat), 11mg chol., 553mg sod., 41g carb. (5g sugars, 1g fiber), 4g pro.

HERBED BREAD TWISTS

A blend of herbs and a special shape dress up ordinary frozen bread dough in this unbelievably easy recipe.

—Deb Stapert, Comstock Park, MI

PREP: 30 MIN. + RISING • BAKE: 10 MIN. • MAKES: 2 DOZEN

¼ **cup butter, softened**
¼ **tsp. garlic powder**
¼ **tsp. each dried basil, marjoram and oregano**
1 **loaf (1 lb.) frozen bread dough, thawed**
¾ **cup shredded part-skim mozzarella cheese**
1 **large egg**
1 **Tbsp. water**
4 **tsp. sesame seeds**

1. In a small bowl, combine butter and seasonings. On a lightly floured surface, roll dough into a 12-in. square. Spread with butter mixture to within ½ in. of edges; sprinkle with cheese.

2. Fold dough into thirds. Cut widthwise into 24 strips. Twist each strip twice; pinch ends to seal. Place 2 in. apart on greased baking sheets. Cover and let rise in a warm place until doubled, about 40 minutes.

3. Beat egg and water; brush over dough. Sprinkle with sesame seeds. Bake at 375° until light golden brown, 10-12 minutes. Remove from pans to wire racks.

1 TWIST: 84 cal., 4g tat (2g sat. fat), 17mg chol., 140mg sod., 10g carb. (1g sugars, 1g fiber), 3g pro.

MUENSTER BREAD

This recipe makes a beautiful round loaf. With a layer of cheese peeking out of every slice, it's definitely worth the effort.

—Melanie Mero, Ida, MI

PREP: 20 MIN. + RISING • **BAKE:** 40 MIN. + COOLING • **MAKES:** 1 LOAF (16 SLICES)

2 pkg. (¼ oz. each) active dry yeast
1 cup warm 2% milk (110° to 115°)
½ cup butter, softened
2 Tbsp. sugar
1 tsp. salt
3¼ to 3¾ cups all-purpose flour
1 large egg plus 1 large egg yolk, room temperature
4 cups shredded Muenster cheese
1 large egg white, beaten

1. In a large bowl, dissolve yeast in milk. Add the softened butter, sugar, salt and 2 cups flour; beat until smooth. Stir in enough remaining flour to form a soft dough.

2. Turn onto a floured surface; knead until smooth and elastic, 6-8 minutes. Place in a greased bowl, turning once to grease top. Cover and let rise in a warm place until doubled, about 1 hour.

3. In a large bowl, beat egg and yolk; stir in cheese. Punch down dough; roll into a 16-in. circle.

4. Place in a greased 10-in. cast-iron skillet or 9-in. round baking pan, letting dough drape over the edges. Spoon the cheese mixture into center of dough. Gather dough up over filling in 1½-in. pleats. Gently squeeze pleats together at top and twist to make a topknot. Let rise 10-15 minutes.

5. Brush loaf with egg white. Bake at 375° for 40-45 minutes. Cool on a wire rack for 20 minutes. Serve warm.

1 SLICE: 273 cal., 16g fat (9g sat. fat), 71mg chol., 399mg sod., 22g carb. (3g sugars, 1g fiber), 11g pro.

BLUE
RIBBON
WINNER

CROWD-PLEASING SNACKS

Whether you need a munchie for movie night, a quick nibble between meals or an impressive appetizer for holiday parties, you'll find the perfect bites and beverages here.

BARBECUED MEATBALLS

Grape jelly and chili sauce are the secrets that make these meatballs so fantastic. If I'm serving them at a party, I prepare the meatballs and sauce in advance and reheat them right before guests arrive.

—*Irma Schnuelle, Manitowoc, WI*

PREP: 20 MIN. • COOK: 15 MIN. • MAKES: ABOUT 3 DOZEN

½ cup dry bread crumbs
⅓ cup finely chopped onion
¼ cup 2% milk
1 large egg, lightly beaten
1 Tbsp. minced fresh parsley
1 tsp. salt
1 tsp. Worcestershire sauce
½ tsp. pepper
1 lb. lean ground beef (90% lean)
¼ cup canola oil
1 bottle (12 oz.) chili sauce
1 jar (10 oz.) grape jelly

1. In a large bowl, combine the first 8 ingredients. Crumble beef over mixture and mix lightly but thoroughly. Shape into 1-in. balls. In a large skillet, brown meatballs in oil on all sides.

2. Remove meatballs and drain. In the same skillet, combine chili sauce and jelly; cook and stir over medium heat until jelly has melted. Return meatballs to pan; heat through.

1 MEATBALL: 71 cal., 3g fat (1g sat. fat), 13mg chol., 215mg sod., 9g carb. (7g sugars, 0 fiber), 3g pro.

CARAMELIZED HAM & SWISS BUNS

My next-door neighbor shared this recipe with me, and I simply cannot improve it!
You can make it ahead and cook it quickly when company arrives. It's so delicious.

—Iris Weihemuller, Baxter, MN

PREP: 25 MIN. + CHILLING • BAKE: 30 MIN. • MAKES: 1 DOZEN

1 pkg. (18 oz.) Hawaiian
  sweet rolls
½ cup horseradish sauce
¾ lb. sliced deli ham
6 slices Swiss
  cheese, halved
½ cup butter, cubed
2 Tbsp. finely
  chopped onion
2 Tbsp. brown sugar
1 Tbsp. spicy brown
  mustard
2 tsp. poppy seeds
1¼ tsp. Worcestershire
  sauce
¼ tsp. garlic powder

1. Spread cut side of roll bottoms with horseradish sauce. Layer with ham and cheese; replace tops. Arrange in a single layer in a greased 13x9-in. baking pan.

2. In a small skillet, heat butter over medium-high heat. Add the onion; cook and stir 1-2 minutes or until tender. Stir in remaining ingredients. Pour over rolls. Refrigerate, covered, several hours or overnight.

3. Preheat oven to 350°. Bake, covered, 25 minutes. Bake, uncovered, 5-10 minutes longer or until golden brown.

1 SANDWICH: 315 cal., 17g fat (9g sat. fat), 61mg chol., 555mg sod., 29g carb. (13g sugars, 2g fiber), 13g pro.

KITCHEN TIP: It's easy to turn this sandwich into a Reuben. Swap in corned beef or pastrami for the ham, add a layer of sauerkraut, and substitute caraway seeds for the poppy.

HONEY HORSERADISH DIP

We love having appetizers on Friday night instead of a meal, and during the summer we enjoy cooler foods. This has just the right amount of zing.

—Ann Marie Eberhart, Gig Harbor, WA

PREP: 10 MIN. + CHILLING • MAKES: 1 CUP

½ cup fat-free plain
   Greek yogurt
¼ cup stone-ground
   mustard
¼ cup honey
2 Tbsp. prepared
   horseradish
   Cold cooked shrimp and
   fresh sugar snap peas

Combine yogurt, mustard, honey and horseradish; refrigerate 1 hour. Serve with shrimp and snap peas.

2 TBSP.: 54 cal., 1g fat (0 sat. fat), 0 chol., 177mg sod., 11g carb. (10g sugars, 0 fiber), 2g pro.

DIABETIC EXCHANGES: 1 starch.

LIVING IN THE LAND OF MILK & EGGNOG

BY CASEY SCHOCH HILLSBORO, OREGON

The holidays are extra special (and extra busy) at Schoch Dairy and Creamery, an 80-acre dairy farm in the Pacific Northwest. My husband, Dave, grew up on this farm, which his parents purchased in 1966. Now, Dave and I, along with our four sons, Jake, Nate, Sam and Ben, happily live and work here.

Originally our farm operated as a conventional dairy. We milked 200 cows twice a day and all the milk was shipped to a dairy cooperative. As milk prices fluctuated, however, my husband and I searched for ways to make our dairy and business more profitable and consistent. As a family, we began to reimagine how our farm might operate. We looked at ways we could work together to make that happen.

We started processing our own milk and selling it in bottles directly to our local community. We launched Schoch Dairy and Creamery in 2015, and we have never looked back.

Customers come out to the farm to buy milk and visit with our cows all year. When the holidays begin, though, they come for eggnog.

A family favorite, our eggnog is creamy and delicious. Making flavored milk is a labor of love, but the aroma of the eggnog ingredients blending is heavenly! Customers smile as they pick it up for Christmas, and bottles disappear from the cooler as fast as we can stock them.

Growing up on a dairy farm is a lot of hard work but also provides opportunities and freedoms that others may never experience. Our sons are truly friends, and wherever life may take them, they will always share the common bond of working together as a family at our dairy and creamery.

Top: Dave and Casey stroll the farm with sons Jake, Ben, Sam and Nate. Both Nate and Sam attend Oregon State University, but they're able to come home and help out during winter break. Bottom: Dave and Casey check on a batch of eggnog.

Top: Sam and Ben help with feeding time. Bottom left: Everyone pitches in to bottle up the season's very last batch of eggnog.
Bottom right: Try making your own with the recipe for Homemade Eggnog on page 111.

HOMEMADE EGGNOG

After just one taste, folks will know this homemade
holiday treat is a special way to celebrate.

—Pat Waymire, Yellow Springs, OH

PREP: 15 MIN. • COOK: 30 MIN. + CHILLING • MAKES: 12 SERVINGS (3 QT.)

12 large eggs
1½ cups sugar
½ tsp. salt
8 cups whole milk, divided
2 Tbsp. vanilla extract
1 tsp. ground nutmeg
2 cups heavy
   whipping cream
   Additional nutmeg,
   optional

1. In a heavy saucepan, whisk together eggs, sugar and salt. Gradually add 4 cups milk; cook and stir over low heat until a thermometer reads 160°-170°, 30-35 minutes. Do not allow to boil. Immediately transfer to a large bowl.

2. Stir in vanilla, nutmeg and remaining milk. Place bowl in an ice-water bath, stirring until milk mixture is cool. (If mixture separates, process in a blender until smooth.) Refrigerate, covered, until cold, at least 3 hours.

3. To serve, beat cream until soft peaks form. Whisk gently into cooled milk mixture. If desired, sprinkle with additional nutmeg before serving.

1 CUP: 411 cal., 25g fat (14g sat. fat), 247mg chol., 251mg sod., 35g carb. (35g sugars, 0 fiber), 13g pro.

KITCHEN TIPS: Eggnog may be stored, covered, in the refrigerator for several days. Whisk it before serving. If you're entertaining the 21-and-over crowd, spike this easy eggnog recipe with bourbon or dark rum.

ASPARAGUS BRUSCHETTA

I really like asparagus, so I'm always trying it in different things.
This is a delicious twist on traditional bruschetta.

—Elaine Sweet, Dallas, TX

TAKES: 30 MIN. • MAKES: 1 DOZEN

3 cups water
½ lb. fresh asparagus,
   trimmed and cut
   into ½-in. pieces
2 cups grape
   tomatoes, halved
¼ cup minced fresh basil
3 green onions, chopped
3 Tbsp. lime juice
1 Tbsp. olive oil
3 garlic cloves, minced
1½ tsp. grated lime zest
¼ tsp. salt
¼ tsp. pepper
12 slices French bread
   baguette (½ in.
   thick), toasted
½ cup crumbled
   blue cheese

1. In a large saucepan, bring water to a boil. Add the asparagus; cover and boil for 2-4 minutes. Drain and immediately place the asparagus in ice water. Drain and pat dry.

2. In a large bowl, combine the asparagus, tomatoes, basil, onions, lime juice, oil, garlic, lime zest, salt and pepper. Using a slotted spoon, spoon asparagus mixture onto bread. Sprinkle with blue cheese.

1 PIECE: 88 cal., 3g fat (1g sat. fat), 4mg chol., 237mg sod., 13g carb. (1g sugars, 1g fiber), 3g pro.

DIABETIC EXCHANGES: 1 starch, ½ fat.

DEVILED EGGS WITH BACON

These yummy deviled eggs went over so well at our summer cookouts, I started making them for holiday dinners, too. Everyone likes the addition of crumbled bacon.

—*Barbara Reid, Mounds, OK*

TAKES: 30 MIN. • **MAKES:** 2 DOZEN

12 hard-boiled large eggs
⅓ cup mayonnaise
3 bacon strips, cooked and crumbled
3 Tbsp. finely chopped red onion
3 Tbsp. sweet pickle relish
¼ tsp. smoked paprika

Cut eggs in half lengthwise. Remove yolks; set whites aside. In a small bowl, mash yolks. Add the mayonnaise, bacon, onion and relish; mix well. Stuff into egg whites. Refrigerate until serving. Sprinkle with paprika.

1 STUFFED EGG HALF: 68 cal., 5g fat (1g sat. fat), 108mg chol., 82mg sod., 1g carb. (1g sugars, 0 fiber), 3g pro.

HARVEST APPLE CIDER

I simmer this comforting cider in my slow cooker every fall. It's a wonderful way to warm up once afternoon chores are done, and it's a great way to welcome guests to your home.
—*Lesley Geisel, Severna Park, MD*

PREP: 5 MIN. • **COOK:** 2 HOURS • **MAKES:** ABOUT 2 QT.

8   whole cloves
4   cups apple cider or juice
4   cups pineapple juice
½   cup water
1   cinnamon stick (3 in.)
1   tea bag

1. Place cloves on a double thickness of cheesecloth; bring up corners of cloth and tie with kitchen string to form a bag. Place the remaining ingredients in a 3-qt. slow cooker; add spice bag.

2. Cover and cook on low for 2 hours or until cider reaches desired temperature. Discard spice bag, cinnamon stick and tea bag before serving.

1 CUP: 130 cal., 0 fat (0 sat. fat), 0 chol., 14mg sod., 32g carb. (30g sugars, 0 fiber), 0 pro.

STRAWBERRY SALSA

This deliciously different salsa is versatile, fresh-tasting and colorful. People are surprised to see a salsa made with strawberries, but it's excellent with corn chips or spooned over grilled chicken.

—Jean Giroux, Belchertown, MA

PREP: 15 MIN. + CHILLING • MAKES: 4 CUPS

- 1 pint fresh strawberries, chopped
- 4 plum tomatoes, seeded and chopped
- 1 small red onion, finely chopped
- 1 to 2 medium jalapeno peppers, minced
- 2 Tbsp. lime juice
- 1 Tbsp. olive oil
- 2 garlic cloves, minced
  Tortilla chips

In a large bowl, combine the strawberries, tomatoes, onion and jalapenos. Stir in lime juice, oil and garlic. Cover and refrigerate for 2 hours. Serve with tortilla chips.

¼ CUP: 19 cal., 1g fat (0 sat. fat), 0 chol., 1mg sod., 3g carb. (2g sugars, 1g fiber), 0 pro.

DIABETIC EXCHANGES: Free food.

BLUE RIBBON WINNER

NUTELLA HAND PIES

These pint-size Nutella hand pies made with puff pastry are too good to keep to yourself!
Call your big and little kids to the kitchen for a snack they'll never forget.
—Taste of Home *Test Kitchen*

TAKES: 30 MIN. • MAKES: 9 SERVINGS

1 large egg
1 Tbsp. water
1 sheet frozen puff
   pastry, thawed
3 Tbsp. Nutella
1 to 2 tsp. grated
   orange zest

ICING
⅓ cup confectioners' sugar
½ tsp. orange juice
⅛ tsp. grated orange zest
   Additional Nutella,
   optional

1. Preheat oven to 400°. In a small bowl, whisk egg with water.

2. Unfold puff pastry; cut into 9 squares. Place 1 tsp. Nutella in center of each; sprinkle with orange zest. Brush edges of pastry with egg mixture. Fold 1 corner over filling to form a triangle; press edges to seal. Transfer to an ungreased baking sheet.

3. Bake for 17-20 minutes or until pastry is golden brown and cooked through. Cool slightly.

4. In a small bowl, mix confectioners' sugar, orange juice and orange zest; drizzle over pies. If desired, warm additional Nutella in a microwave and drizzle over tops.

1 HAND PIE: 190 cal., 10g fat (2g sat. fat), 21mg chol., 100mg sod., 24g carb. (8g sugars, 2g fiber), 3g pro.

BACON-WRAPPED SWEET POTATO BITES

After making little bacon-wrapped sausages for years, I needed a change! I had an extra sweet potato and half a package of bacon on hand, so I put on my thinking cap and came up with this appetizer.

—*Kelly Williams, Forked River, NJ*

PREP: 25 MIN. • **BAKE:** 40 MIN. • **MAKES:** ABOUT 2½ DOZEN

2 **Tbsp. butter, melted**
½ **tsp. salt**
½ **tsp. cayenne pepper**
¼ **tsp. ground cinnamon**
2 **large sweet potatoes (about 1¾ lbs.), peeled and cut into 1-in. cubes**
1 **lb. bacon strips, halved**
¼ **cup packed brown sugar Maple syrup, warmed**

1. Preheat oven to 350°. In a large bowl, mix butter and seasonings. Add sweet potatoes and toss to coat.

2. Wrap 1 piece bacon around each sweet potato cube; secure with a toothpick. Sprinkle with brown sugar. Place bites on a parchment-lined 15x10x1-in. baking pan.

3. Bake 40-45 minutes or until bacon is crisp and sweet potato is tender. Serve with maple syrup.

1 APPETIZER: 60 cal., 3g fat (1g sat. fat), 7mg chol., 136mg sod., 7g carb. (4g sugars, 1g fiber), 2g pro.

OLD-FASHIONED LEMONADE

This sweet-tart lemonade is a traditional part of my Memorial Day and Fourth of July menus. Folks can't get enough of the fresh-squeezed flavor.

—*Tammi Simpson, Greensburg, KY*

PREP: 10 MIN. • COOK: 5 MIN. + CHILLING • MAKES: 7 SERVINGS

1⅓ **cups sugar**
5 **cups water, divided**
1 **Tbsp. grated lemon zest**
1¾ **cups lemon juice (about 10 large lemons)**

In a large saucepan, combine sugar, 1 cup water and lemon zest. Cook and stir over medium heat until sugar is dissolved, about 4 minutes. Remove from heat. Stir in lemon juice and remaining water; refrigerate until cold. Serve over ice.

1 CUP: 142 cal., 0 fat (0 sat. fat), 0 chol., 1mg sod., 37g carb. (35g sugars, 0 fiber), 0 pro.

KITCHEN TIPS: To make limeade, substitute lime zest for lemon zest and limes for lemons. To make lavender lemonade, add 2 Tbsp. dried lavender to the sugar and lemon zest mixture before simmering. If desired, strain before serving. To make ginger-mint lemonade, add 1-2 Tbsp. grated fresh gingerroot and 1-2 mint sprigs to the sugar and lemon zest mixture before simmering. If desired, strain before serving.

GRILLED CHERRY-GLAZED CHICKEN WINGS

When I take these grilled wings to events, there are never any leftovers!
Friends and family love them, and I love the zesty homemade glaze.

—Ashley Gable, Atlanta, GA

PREP: 20 MIN. • GRILL: 15 MIN. • MAKES: 1 DOZEN

12 chicken wings
    (about 3 lbs.)
3 Tbsp. canola oil, divided
1 garlic clove, minced
1 cup ketchup
½ cup cider vinegar
½ cup cherry preserves
2 Tbsp. Louisiana-
    style hot sauce
1 Tbsp. Worcestershire
    sauce
3 tsp. coarse salt, divided
1 tsp. coarsely ground
    pepper, divided

1. Using a sharp knife, cut through the 2 wing joints; discard wing tips. In a small saucepan, heat 1 Tbsp. oil over medium heat. Add garlic; cook and stir 1 minute. Stir in ketchup, vinegar, preserves, hot sauce, Worcestershire sauce, 1 tsp. salt and ½ tsp. pepper. Cook and stir until heated through. Brush wings with remaining oil; sprinkle with remaining salt and pepper.

2. Grill, covered, over medium heat 15-18 minutes or until juices run clear, turning occasionally and brushing with glaze during the last 5 minutes of grilling. Serve with remaining glaze.

1 CHICKEN WING: 214 cal., 12g fat (3g sat fat), 36mg chol., 867mg sod., 15g carb. (14g sugars, 0g fiber), 12g pro.

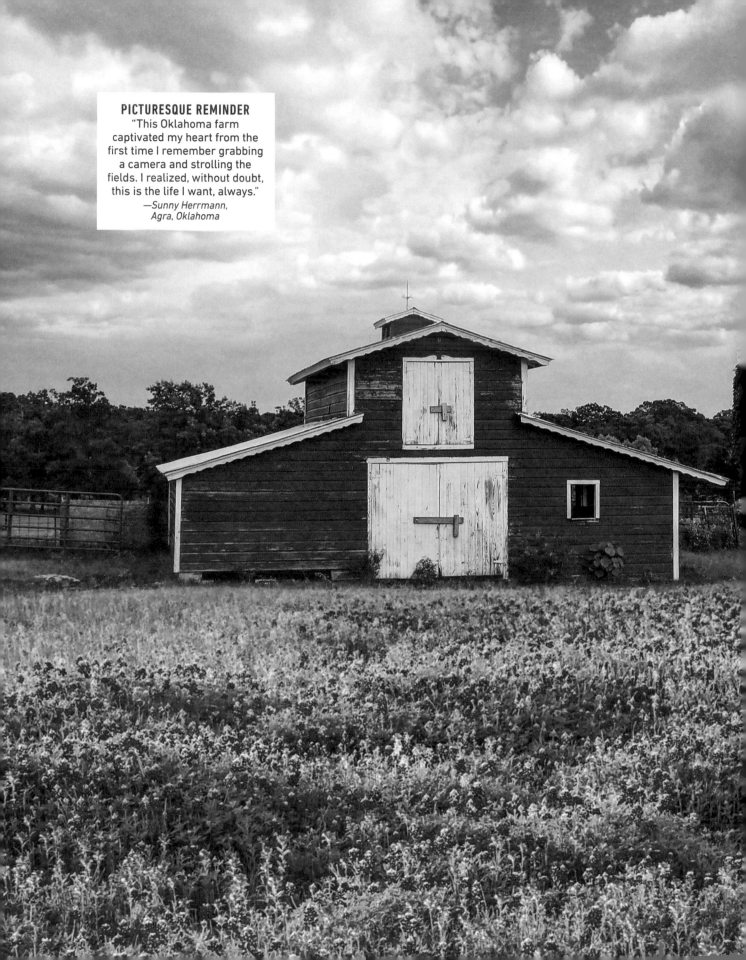

PICTURESQUE REMINDER
"This Oklahoma farm captivated my heart from the first time I remember grabbing a camera and strolling the fields. I realized, without doubt, this is the life I want, always."
—*Sunny Herrmann,*
Agra, Oklahoma

FROM TOP:

EASY RIDER

"Cooper, our Labrador retriever, sat in the back of our '52 Chevy enjoying the sunshine when I took this photo one morning. He may not look too impressed—he's used to me taking pictures of him. Cooper is a farm dog and loves to ride in the truck."

—*Ashley Ford, Hamilton, Missouri*

LOOK-ALIKES?

My daughter Adeline and this goat seem to have the same expression, and her pigtails match the goat's ears.

—*Jessica Roberts, Camarillo, California*

HEIRLOOM TOMATO GALETTE WITH PECORINO

I found beautiful heirloom tomatoes and had to show them off. In this easy galette, the tomatoes are tangy and the crust is beyond buttery.

—*Jessica Chang, Playa Vista, CA*

PREP: 10 MIN. + CHILLING • **BAKE:** 25 MIN. + COOLING • **MAKES:** 6 SERVINGS

1 cup all-purpose flour
1 tsp. baking powder
¾ tsp. kosher salt, divided
½ cup cold unsalted butter, cubed
½ cup sour cream
2 cups cherry tomatoes, halved
3 oz. Pecorino Romano cheese, thinly sliced

1. Whisk flour, baking powder and ½ tsp. salt; cut in butter until mixture resembles coarse crumbs. Stir in sour cream until dough forms a ball. Shape into a disk; cover and refrigerate until firm enough to roll, about 2 hours.

2. Meanwhile, place tomatoes in a colander; toss with remaining salt. Let stand 15 minutes.

3. Preheat oven to 425°. On a floured sheet of parchment, roll dough into a 12-in. circle. Transfer to a baking sheet.

4. Place cheese slices over crust to within 2 in. of edge; arrange tomatoes over cheese. Fold crust edges over filling, pleating as you go and leaving center uncovered. Bake until crust is golden brown and cheese is bubbly, about 25 minutes. Cool 10 minutes before slicing.

1 SLICE: 317 cal., 23g fat (15g sat. fat), 68mg chol., 559mg sod., 19g carb. (2g sugars, 1g fiber), 9g pro.

BLUE
RIBBON
WINNER

CHEESY SAUSAGE STROMBOLI

Perfect for an evening snack or light lunch, these sausage-filled loaves
are easy. Best of all, I never have to worry about storing leftovers!

—Vada McRoberts, Silver Lake, KS

PREP: 30 MIN. + RISING • BAKE: 20 MIN. • MAKES: 2 LOAVES (16 SLICES EACH)

5 cups all-purpose flour
2 Tbsp. sugar
2 tsp. salt
2 pkg. (¼ oz. each)
   active dry yeast
1½ cups warm water
   (120° to 130°)
½ cup warm 2% milk
   (120° to 130°)
2 Tbsp. butter, melted
2 lbs. bulk pork sausage
4 cups shredded part-skim
   mozzarella cheese
3 large eggs, divided use
1 tsp. minced fresh basil
   or ¼ tsp. dried basil
2 Tbsp. grated
   Parmesan cheese

1. In a large bowl, combine the flour, sugar, salt and yeast. Add water, milk and butter; beat on low until well combined.

2. Turn onto a well-floured surface; knead until smooth and elastic, 6-8 minutes. Place in a greased bowl, turning once to grease top. Cover and let rise in a warm place until doubled, about 1 hour.

3. Meanwhile, in a large skillet over medium-high heat, cook the sausage until no longer pink; drain and cool. Stir in the mozzarella, 2 eggs and basil; set aside.

4. Punch the dough down; divide in half. Roll 1 portion into a 15x10-in. rectangle on a greased baking sheet. Spoon half of the sausage mixture lengthwise down 1 side of rectangle to within 1 in. of edges.

5. Fold dough over filling; pinch edges to seal. Cut 4 diagonal slits on top of stromboli. Repeat with remaining dough and filling. Beat remaining egg; brush over loaves. Sprinkle with Parmesan cheese. Cover and let rise until doubled, about 45 minutes.

6. Bake at 375° for 20-25 minutes or until golden brown. Slice; serve warm.

1 SLICE: 370 cal., 18g fat (8g sat. fat), 82mg chol., 702mg sod., 34g carb. (4g sugars, 1g fiber), 17g pro.

FRIED ASPARAGUS

This battered asparagus is a favorite at all of our events. The crispy bites are fun to eat with a simple side of ranch dressing for dipping.

—Lori Kimble, Montgomery, AL

TAKES: 30 MIN. • MAKES: 2½ DOZEN

1 cup all-purpose flour
¾ cup cornstarch
1¼ tsp. salt
1¼ tsp. baking powder
¾ tsp. baking soda
¾ tsp. garlic salt
½ tsp. pepper
1 cup beer or nonalcoholic beer
3 large egg whites
2½ lbs. fresh asparagus, trimmed
Oil for deep-fat frying
Ranch salad dressing

1. In a large bowl, combine the first 7 ingredients. Combine beer and egg whites; stir into dry ingredients just until moistened. Dip asparagus into batter.

2. In a deep cast-iron or electric skillet, heat 1½ in. oil to 375°. Fry asparagus in batches until golden brown, 2-3 minutes on each side. Drain on paper towels. Serve immediately with the ranch dressing.

1 PIECE: 70 cal., 4g fat (0 sat. fat), 0 chol., 207mg sod., 7g carb. (1g sugars, 0 fiber), 1g pro.

KITCHEN TIP: Out of garlic salt? Combine 1 tsp. garlic powder with 3 tsp. of table salt or other fine-grained salt. The ratio works the same for onion salt as well.

HOT CHEESE DIP

When a colleague brought this quick and cheesy dip to school for a teachers' potluck,
I immediately gave it an A+. I had to have this irresistibly creamy recipe!

—*Ardyce Piehl, Poynette, WI*

TAKES: 30 MIN. • MAKES: 3 CUPS

2 cups shredded part-skim
mozzarella cheese

2 cups shredded
cheddar cheese

2 cups mayonnaise

1 medium onion, minced

1 can (4 to 4½ oz.) chopped
green chiles, drained

½ cup sliced ripe olives

1½ oz. sliced pepperoni
Assorted crackers and
fresh vegetables

Preheat oven to 325°. Combine the first 5 ingredients; spread
into a greased shallow baking dish or pie plate. Top with olives
and pepperoni. Bake until bubbly, about 25 minutes. Serve with
crackers and fresh vegetables.

2 TBSP.: 201 cal., 19g fat (5g sat. fat), 18mg chol., 285mg sod., 2g
carb. (0 sugars, 0 fiber), 5g pro.

BLUE
RIBBON
WINNER

CHAPTER 5

COUNTRY-KISSED SIDE DISHES

Add a touch of garden-fresh goodness to your table with a delectable side. From vibrant green-bean salads to golden potato bakes, turn here for dinner additions that will round out any menu.

MAPLE-GINGER GLAZED CARROTS

I first made this dish for my family and friends one Thanksgiving.
Not only are the carrots lovely on any table, but they taste terrific, too.
—*Jannette Sabo, Lexington Park, MD*

PREP: 15 MIN. • COOK: 25 MIN. • MAKES: 16 SERVINGS

4 lbs. medium carrots,
   cut into ¼-in. slices
¼ cup water
3 Tbsp. butter, divided
1 Tbsp. minced fresh
   gingerroot
⅓ cup maple syrup
1 Tbsp. cider vinegar
½ tsp. salt
¼ tsp. pepper
   Minced fresh parsley,
   optional

1. In a Dutch oven, combine the carrots, water, 2 Tbsp. butter and ginger. Cover and cook for 10 minutes. Cook, uncovered, until carrots are crisp-tender, 6-8 minutes longer.

2. Stir in the syrup, vinegar, salt and pepper. Cook, stirring frequently, until sauce is thickened, 5-6 minutes. Stir in remaining butter. If desired, garnish with parsley.

¾ CUP: 83 cal., 2g fat (1g sat. fat), 6mg chol., 168mg sod., 15g carb. (9g sugars, 3g fiber), 1g pro.

DIABETIC EXCHANGES: 2 vegetable, ½ fat.

SPRING ASPARAGUS

This fresh and colorful side dish is delicious served warm or cold.
I get lots of compliments on the homemade dressing.

—*Millie Vickery, Lena, IL*

TAKES: 25 MIN. • MAKES: 8 SERVINGS

1½ lbs. fresh asparagus,
   trimmed and cut
   into 2-in. pieces
2 small tomatoes,
   cut into wedges
3 Tbsp. cider vinegar
¾ tsp. Worcestershire
   sauce
⅓ cup sugar
1 Tbsp. grated onion
½ tsp. salt
½ tsp. paprika
⅓ cup canola oil
¼ cup sliced almonds,
   toasted
⅓ cup crumbled blue
   cheese, optional

1. In a large saucepan, bring 1 cup water to a boil. Add the asparagus; cook, covered, until crisp-tender, 3-5 minutes. Drain; place in a large bowl. Add the tomatoes; cover and keep warm.

2. Place vinegar, Worcestershire sauce, sugar, onion, salt and paprika in a blender; cover and process until smooth. While processing, gradually add oil in a steady stream. Toss with asparagus mixture. Top with almonds and, if desired, cheese.

¾ CUP: 154 cal., 11g fat (1g sat. fat), 0 chol., 159mg sod., 12g carb. (10g sugars, 1g fiber), 2g pro.

DIABETIC EXCHANGES: 2 fat, 1 vegetable, ½ starch.

FRIED ONIONS & APPLES

Since a lot of flavorful onions are grown in our state, they are always part of my menu. This tangy side dish is good with pork and beef. The inspiration for this dish was a prolific apple tree.

—*Janice Mitchell, Aurora, CO*

TAKES: 30 MIN. • MAKES: 12 SERVINGS

3   large yellow
    onions, sliced
3   Tbsp. butter
6   large tart red
    apples, sliced
½   cup packed brown sugar
1   tsp. salt
½   tsp. paprika
⅛   tsp. ground nutmeg

1. In a large cast-iron or other heavy skillet, saute onions in butter until tender. Place apples on top of onions. Combine remaining ingredients; sprinkle over apples.

2. Cover and simmer for 10 minutes. Uncover and simmer until apples are tender, 5 minutes longer. Serve with a slotted spoon.

1 CUP: 137 cal., 3g fat (2g sat. fat), 8mg chol., 230mg sod., 28g carb. (24g sugars, 4g fiber), 1g pro.

ROSEMARY ROOT VEGETABLES

This heartwarming side dish is sure to get rave reviews! Although the ingredient list may look long, you'll soon see that this colorful medley is a snap to prepare.

—Taste of Home *Test Kitchen*

PREP: 20 MIN. • BAKE: 20 MIN. • MAKES: 10 SERVINGS

1 **small rutabaga, peeled and chopped**

1 **medium sweet potato, peeled and chopped**

2 **medium parsnips, peeled and chopped**

1 **medium turnip, peeled and chopped**

¼ **lb. fresh Brussels sprouts, halved**

2 **Tbsp. olive oil**

2 **Tbsp. minced fresh rosemary or 2 tsp. dried rosemary, crushed**

1 **tsp. minced garlic**

½ **tsp. salt**

½ **tsp. pepper**

Preheat oven to 425°. Place the vegetables in a large bowl. In a small bowl, combine oil, rosemary, garlic, salt and pepper. Pour over vegetables; toss to coat. Arrange vegetables in a single layer in two 15x10x1-in. baking pans coated with cooking spray. Bake, uncovered, stirring once, until tender, 20-25 minutes.

¾ CUP: 78 cal., 3g fat (0 sat. fat), 0 chol., 137mg sod., 13g carb. (5g sugars, 3g fiber), 1g pro.

DIABETIC EXCHANGES: 1 starch, ½ fat.

CHEESE SMASHED POTATOES

Who doesn't like mashed potatoes? Try this incredible version with any entree.
Leaving the potato skins on adds a touch of color and speeds up preparation.

—Janet Homes, Surprise, AZ

PREP: 10 MIN. • **COOK:** 25 MIN. • **MAKES:** 4 SERVINGS

1 lb. small red potatoes,
   quartered
1 cup fresh cauliflowerets
⅔ cup shredded
   reduced-fat
   cheddar cheese
¼ cup reduced-fat
   sour cream
¼ tsp. salt

1. Place potatoes in a large saucepan and cover with water. Bring to a boil. Reduce heat; cover and cook 10 minutes. Add cauliflower; cook until vegetables are tender, 10 minutes longer.

2. Drain; mash with cheese, sour cream and salt.

¾ CUP: 161 cal., 5g fat (3g sat. fat), 18mg chol., 292mg sod., 21g carb. (3g sugars, 3g fiber), 8g pro.

DIABETIC EXCHANGES: 1 starch, 1 medium-fat meat.

GOING GREEN

STORY & PHOTOS BY JAEMOR FARMS ALTO, GEORGIA

On 500 acres of farmland in the foothills of the Appalachian Mountains, Jimmy Echols and his family grow a wide variety of produce, including apples, peaches, berries, squash, zucchini, pumpkins and beans.

With his adult children and grandchildren, Jimmy is following the path taken by his grandfather, Tim Echols, who began this farm with cotton and a few peach trees in 1912. The peach orchards are the heart of today's business, since the cooler mountain air makes it possible to grow certain varieties unique to the state.

Meeting customer demand has been central to the farm's success, says marketing coordinator Caroline Lewallen. In addition to peaches, that demand includes a stringless snap bean variety called the Blue Lake Bush bean, as well as white half-runner beans, which Caroline calls an "easy-to-grow heirloom treasure."

White half-runners are the most popular green bean in the north Georgia mountains, according to Jaemor's website. They provide a greater yield than a traditional pole bean, and for this reason, says Caroline, they were commonplace in many Depression-era gardens. Nowadays, customers buy them from Jaemor by the bushel for canning or cooking fresh.

Fall is an especially active time on the farm, as the family offers autumn visitors a corn maze and pumpkin fields to explore. And although the bean-growing season is over come November, Jaemor Farms continues to sell its south Georgia pecans and other homegrown products at its year-round market in Alto.

The Echols family built its permanent market building in 1981 after years of roadside stand sales. Now more than 1 million guests visit annually, loading up on green beans as well as those glorious peaches.

Left: Jimmy Echols and his great-granddaughter Chloe, who represent the farm's third and sixth generations. Above: Fresh white half-runner beans and Southern Green Beans with Apricots (recipe on page 150).

SOUTHERN GREEN BEANS WITH APRICOTS

Green beans and apricots have become a family tradition at our house.
Enhanced with balsamic vinegar, the flavors will make your taste buds pop.

—Ashley Davis, Easley, SC

PREP: 15 MIN. • COOK: 20 MIN. • MAKES: 8 SERVINGS

2 lbs. fresh green
beans, trimmed
1 can (14½ oz.)
chicken broth
½ lb. bacon strips, chopped
1 cup dried apricots,
chopped
¼ cup balsamic vinegar
¾ tsp. salt
¾ tsp. garlic powder
¾ tsp. pepper

1. Place beans and broth in a large saucepan. Bring to a boil. Cook, covered, until beans are crisp-tender, 4-7 minutes; drain.

2. In a large skillet, cook bacon over medium heat until crisp, stirring occasionally. Remove with a slotted spoon; drain on paper towels. Discard drippings, reserving 1 Tbsp. drippings in pan.

3. Add apricots to drippings; cook and stir over medium heat until softened. Stir in vinegar, salt, garlic powder, pepper and beans; cook and stir until beans are coated, 2-3 minutes longer. Sprinkle with bacon.

¾ CUP: 149 cal., 6g fat (2g sat. fat), 12mg chol., 464mg sod., 21g carb. (14g sugars, 5g fiber), 6g pro.

MARINA'S GOLDEN CORN FRITTERS

Just one bite of these fritters takes me back to when my kids were young. Nowadays for our get-togethers, I sometimes triple the recipe. Serve the fritters with maple syrup or agave nectar.

—*Marina Castle Kelley, Canyon Country, CA*

TAKES: 30 MIN. • MAKES: 32 FRITTERS

2½ cups all-purpose flour
3 tsp. baking powder
2 tsp. dried parsley flakes
1 tsp. salt
2 large eggs, room temperature
¾ cup 2% milk
2 Tbsp. butter, melted
2 tsp. grated onion
1 can (15¼ oz.) whole kernel corn, drained
Oil for deep-fat frying

1. In a large bowl, whisk flour, baking powder, parsley and salt. In another bowl, whisk eggs, milk, melted butter and onion until blended. Add to dry ingredients, stirring just until moistened. Fold in corn.

2. In an electric skillet or deep fryer, heat oil to 375°. Drop batter by tablespoonfuls, several at a time, into hot oil. Fry 2-3 minutes on each side or until golden brown. Drain on paper towels.

2 FRITTERS: 162 cal., 8g fat (2g sat. fat), 28mg chol., 327mg sod., 18g carb. (2g sugars, 1g fiber), 4g pro.

BLUE RIBBON WINNER

QUINOA WITH PEAS & ONION

Even picky eaters will love this fresh dish. If you don't have
freshly shelled peas on hand, you can easily substitute frozen.

—Lori Panarella, Phoenixville, PA

PREP: 30 MIN. • COOK: 10 MIN. • MAKES: 6 SERVINGS

2 cups water
1 cup quinoa, rinsed
1 small onion, chopped
1 Tbsp. olive oil
1½ cups frozen peas
½ tsp. salt
¼ tsp. pepper
2 Tbsp. chopped walnuts

1. In a large saucepan, bring water to a boil. Add quinoa. Reduce heat; cover and simmer for 12-15 minutes or until the water is absorbed. Remove from the heat; fluff with a fork.

2. Meanwhile, in a large skillet, saute onion in oil until tender. Add peas; cook and stir until heated through. Stir in the cooked quinoa, salt and pepper. Sprinkle with walnuts.

⅔ CUP: 174 cal., 6g fat (1g sat. fat), 0 chol., 244mg sod., 26g carb. (2g sugars, 4g fiber), 6g pro.

DIABETIC EXCHANGES: 1½ starch, 1 fat.

HOT AND ZESTY QUINOA: Omit peas, salt, pepper and walnuts. Prepare quinoa as directed. Saute onion in oil until tender. Add 3 minced garlic cloves; cook 1 minute. Add 2 cans (10 oz. each) tomatoes and green chiles. Bring to a boil over medium heat. Reduce heat; simmer, uncovered, 10 minutes. Stir in quinoa and ¼ cup chopped marinated quartered artichoke hearts; heat through. Sprinkle with 2 Tbsp. grated Parmesan.

HUSH PUPPIES

Mom is well known for her wonderful hush puppies. Her recipe is easy to prepare and oh, so tasty. The chopped onion adds to the fantastic flavor.

—*Mary McGuire, Graham, NC*

TAKES: 25 MIN. • MAKES: 2 DOZEN

1 cup yellow cornmeal
¼ cup all-purpose flour
1½ tsp. baking powder
½ tsp. salt
1 large egg, room temperature, lightly beaten
¾ cup 2% milk
1 small onion, finely chopped
Oil for deep-fat frying

1. In a large bowl, combine the cornmeal, flour, baking powder and salt. Whisk the egg, milk and onion; add to dry ingredients just until combined.

2. In a cast-iron Dutch oven or an electric skillet, heat oil to 365°. Drop batter by tablespoonfuls into oil. Fry until golden brown, 2-2½ minutes. Drain on paper towels. Serve warm.

1 HUSH PUPPY: 55 cal., 3g fat (0 sat. fat), 9mg chol., 86mg sod., 7g carb. (1g sugars, 0 fiber), 1g pro.

KITCHEN TIP: Deep-frying is a quick process, so make sure you don't overcook or burn your hush puppies by leaving them in the oil too long.

EASY CHEESY LOADED GRITS

A tasty bowl of grits inspired me to develop my own with pork sausage,
green chiles and cheeses. It just might be better than the original.

—*Joan Hallford, North Richland Hills, TX*

PREP: 35 MIN. • **BAKE:** 50 MIN. + STANDING • **MAKES:** 8 SERVINGS

1 lb. mild or spicy bulk
   pork sausage
1 small onion, chopped
4 cups water
½ tsp. salt
1 cup quick-cooking grits
3 cans (4 oz. each)
   chopped green chiles
1½ cups shredded sharp
   cheddar cheese, divided
1½ cups shredded Monterey
   Jack cheese, divided
2 Tbsp. butter
¼ tsp. hot pepper sauce
2 large eggs, lightly beaten
¼ tsp. paprika
   Chopped fresh cilantro

1. Preheat oven to 325°. In a large skillet, cook sausage and onion over medium heat for 6-8 minutes or until sausage is no longer pink, breaking up sausage into crumbles; drain.

2. In a large saucepan, bring water and salt to a boil. Slowly stir in grits. Reduce heat to medium-low; cook, covered, about 5 minutes or until thickened, stirring occasionally. Remove from the heat.

3. Add green chiles, ¾ cup cheddar cheese, ¾ cup Monterey Jack cheese, butter and pepper sauce; stir until cheese is melted. Stir in eggs, then sausage mixture.

4. Transfer to a greased 13x9-in. baking dish. Top with remaining cheeses; sprinkle with paprika. Bake, uncovered, until golden brown and set, 50-60 minutes. Let stand for 10 minutes before serving. Sprinkle with cilantro.

1 CUP: 399 cal., 28g fat (15g sat. fat), 116mg chol., 839mg sod., 19g carb. (2g sugars, 2g fiber), 18g pro.

BLUE
RIBBON
WINNER

BLACK-EYED PEAS WITH COLLARD GREENS

This quick and easy dish has special meaning on New Year's Day, when Southerners eat greens for future wealth and black-eyed peas for prosperity.

—Athena Russell, Greenville, SC

TAKES: 25 MIN. • MAKES: 6 SERVINGS

2 Tbsp. olive oil
1 garlic clove, minced
8 cups chopped
   collard greens
½ tsp. salt
¼ tsp. cayenne pepper
2 cans (15½ oz. each)
   black-eyed peas,
   rinsed and drained
4 plum tomatoes,
   seeded and chopped
¼ cup lemon juice
2 Tbsp. grated
   Parmesan cheese

In a Dutch oven, heat oil over medium heat. Add garlic; cook and stir 1 minute. Add collard greens, salt and cayenne; cook and stir 6-8 minutes or until greens are tender. Add peas, tomatoes and lemon juice; heat through. Sprinkle servings with cheese.

¾ CUP: 177 cal., 5g fat (1g sat. fat), 1mg chol., 412mg sod., 24g carb. (3g sugars, 6g fiber), 9g pro.

ASIAGO MASHED CAULIFLOWER

Asiago and fresh parsley help turn this mashed-potato alternative into a flavorful side dish. What a fast and simple way to use fresh cauliflower.

—Colleen Delawder, Herndon, VA

TAKES: 30 MIN. • MAKES: 4 SERVINGS

1 medium head cauliflower, cut into 1-in. pieces
1 tsp. sea salt, divided
4 oz. cream cheese, softened
½ cup shredded Asiago cheese
2 Tbsp. unsalted butter
2 Tbsp. coarsely chopped fresh parsley
¼ tsp. pepper

1. Place cauliflower and ½ tsp. sea salt in a large saucepan; add water to cover. Bring to a boil. Cook, covered, until very tender, 12-15 minutes. Drain; cool slightly.

2. Transfer to a food processor. Add the cream cheese, Asiago cheese, butter, parsley, pepper and remaining sea salt. Process until blended.

½ CUP: 239 cal., 20g fat (12g sat. fat), 56mg chol., 530mg sod., 10g carb. (4g sugars, 3g fiber), 9g pro.

CLOCKWISE FROM RIGHT:

HIDDEN CHARM
"Colorful leaves perfectly framed the Glade Creek Grist Mill at Babcock State Park in West Virginia."

—*Raymond Massey, Sherburne, New York*

HORSING AROUND
"Our daughter, Addison, loves to visit the horses when spending time at her grandparents' home."

—*Mike and Tricia Jager, Lynden, Washington*

TINY SPROUT
"Though he's just a boy, Peyton has a love for farming. Look into his eyes—you can see a future farmer."

—*Lorri Milton, Friend, Nebraska*

PUMPKIN EATER
"Upon Sadie Mae's first experience with pumpkins, she quickly picked one out to be her jack-o'-lantern."

—*Tami Gingrich, Middlefield, Ohio*

SPICED PICKLED BEETS

With sweet, tangy and spiced flavors, these pickled beets are so good that they'll win over just about everyone in your house. Jars of the colorful beets make great gifts, too!

—Edna Hoffman, Hebron, IN

PREP: 1¼ HOURS • PROCESS: 35 MIN. • MAKES: 4 PINTS

3 **lbs. small fresh beets**
2 **cups sugar**
2 **cups water**
2 **cups cider vinegar**
2 **cinnamon sticks (3 in.)**
1 **tsp. whole cloves**
1 **tsp. whole allspice**

1. Scrub beets and trim tops to 1 in. Place in a Dutch oven and cover with water. Bring to a boil. Reduce heat; cover and simmer until tender, 25-35 minutes. Remove from water; cool. Peel beets and cut into fourths.

2. Place beets in a Dutch oven. Add sugar, water and vinegar. Place the spices on a double thickness of cheesecloth; bring up the corners of the cloth and tie with string to form a bag. Add to beet mixture. Bring to a boil. Reduce heat; cover and simmer 10 minutes. Discard spice bag.

3. Carefully pack beets into 4 hot 1-pint jars to within ½ in. of the top. Carefully ladle hot liquid over beets, leaving ½-in. headspace. Remove air bubbles and adjust headspace, if necessary, by adding hot mixture. Wipe rims. Center lids on jars; screw on bands until fingertip tight.

4. Place jars into canner with simmering water, ensuring that they are completely covered with water. Bring to a boil; process for 35 minutes. Remove jars and cool.

¼ CUP: 53 cal., 0 fat (0 sat. fat), 0 chol., 44mg sod., 12g carb. (11g sugars, 1g fiber), 1g pro.

DIABETIC EXCHANGES: 1 vegetable, ½ starch.

RED POTATOES WITH BEANS

You can serve this homey blend of fresh green beans, potato wedges and chopped red onion hot or cold. Either way, it's a simply delicious addition to any meal.

—Daria Burcar, Rochester, MI

TAKES: 20 MIN. • MAKES: 6 SERVINGS

1⅓ lbs. fresh green
   beans, trimmed
⅓ cup water
6 small red potatoes,
   cut into wedges
½ cup chopped red onion
½ cup Italian salad dressing

1. Place the beans and water in a 2-qt. microwave-safe dish. Cover and microwave on high until tender, 6-8 minutes.

2. Meanwhile, place the potatoes in a large saucepan and cover with water. Bring to a boil. Reduce heat; cover and cook until tender, 10-15 minutes. Drain beans and potatoes; place in a bowl. Add onion and dressing; toss to coat.

¾ CUP: 138 cal., 3g fat (0 sat. fat), 0 chol., 212mg sod., 23g carb. (5g sugars, 5g fiber), 4g pro.

DIABETIC EXCHANGES: 1 starch, 1 vegetable, ½ fat.

TWICE-BAKED SWEET POTATOES WITH BACON

This side always takes my guests by surprise because of the smoky, creamy flavor.
No doubt you'll get major kudos when you place these potatoes on the table.
—*Cynthia Boberskyj, Rochester, NY*

PREP: 20 MIN. • BAKE: 1¼ HOURS • MAKES: 6 SERVINGS

6 medium sweet potatoes
   (about 12 oz. each)
¼ cup butter, softened
½ tsp. salt
⅛ tsp. pepper
2 cups shredded
   cheddar cheese
6 bacon strips, cooked
   and crumbled

1. Preheat oven to 375°. Scrub sweet potatoes; pierce each several times with a fork. Place in a foil-lined 15x10x1-in. baking pan; bake until tender, 1-1¼ hours. Cool slightly.

2. Cut a thin slice off the top of each potato; discard slice. Scoop out pulp, leaving thin shells. In a large bowl, mash pulp with butter, salt and pepper; stir in cheese and bacon. Spoon into potato shells.

3. Return to pan. Bake until heated through, 15-20 minutes.

1 STUFFED POTATO: 611 cal., 24g fat (13g sat. fat), 66mg chol., 683mg sod., 84g carb. (34g sugars, 10g fiber), 17g pro.

ULTIMATE SCALLOPED POTATOES

This tasty variation on traditional scalloped potatoes is
dressed up with garlic, Swiss cheese and Parmesan cheese.
—*Glenda Malan, Lake Forest, CA*

PREP: 20 MIN. + COOLING • BAKE: 1 HOUR • MAKES: 6 SERVINGS

1 tsp. butter, softened
1 cup heavy whipping
   cream
⅓ cup whole milk
1 tsp. salt
½ tsp. pepper
2 garlic cloves, crushed
6 medium potatoes
1 cup shredded
   Swiss cheese
¼ cup shredded
   Parmesan cheese

1. Grease a shallow 13x9-in. baking dish with the butter; set aside. In a small saucepan, combine the cream, milk, salt, pepper and garlic. Cook just until bubbles begin to form around sides of pan. Remove from the heat; cool for 10 minutes.

2. Peel and thinly slice the potatoes; pat dry with paper towels. Layer half the potatoes in prepared baking dish; top with half the cream mixture and half the cheeses. Repeat layers.

3. Bake, covered, at 350° for 40 minutes. Uncover and continue baking until potatoes are tender, 20-25 minutes longer. Let stand for 5-10 minutes before serving.

1 SERVING: 402 cal., 22g fat (14g sat. fat), 77mg chol., 538mg sod., 41g carb. (6g sugars, 3g fiber), 12g pro.

SPICY GRILLED EGGPLANT

This side goes well with any meat you might also be grilling. Thanks to the
Cajun seasoning, the zesty eggplant gets more attention than an ordinary veggie.

—Greg Fontenot, The Woodlands, TX

TAKES: 20 MIN. • MAKES: 8 SERVINGS

2   small eggplants, cut
    into ½-in. slices
¼   cup olive oil
2   Tbsp. lime juice
3   tsp. Cajun seasoning

1. Brush eggplant slices with oil. Drizzle with lime juice; sprinkle
with Cajun seasoning. Let stand 5 minutes.

2. Grill eggplant, covered, over medium heat or broil 4 in. from
heat until tender, 4-5 minutes per side.

1 SERVING: 88 cal., 7g fat (1g sat. fat), 0 chol., 152mg sod., 7g carb.
(3g sugars, 4g fiber), 1g pro.

DIABETIC EXCHANGES. 1½ fat, 1 vegetable.

CHAPTER 6
COMFORTING DINNERS

Call your crew to the table and settle in for the hearty goodness
that country cooking is known for. Fried chicken, cozy casseroles
and beefy staples—they're all here for the taking.

CHICKEN POTPIE CASSEROLE

Here's a comforting family favorite. You can bake your own biscuits for the topping or buy them at the store. I bake a few extra biscuits to eat with butter and jam the next day.

—Liliane Jahnke, Cypress, TX

PREP: 40 MIN. • BAKE: 15 MIN. • MAKES: 8 SERVINGS

⅓ cup butter, cubed
1½ cups sliced fresh
mushrooms
2 medium carrots, sliced
½ medium onion, chopped
¼ cup all-purpose flour
1 cup chicken broth
1 cup 2% milk
4 cups cubed cooked
chicken
1 cup frozen peas
1 jar (2 oz.) diced
pimientos, drained
½ tsp. salt

BISCUIT TOPPING
2 cups all-purpose flour
4 tsp. baking powder
2 tsp. sugar
½ tsp. salt
½ tsp. cream of tartar
½ cup cold butter, cubed
⅔ cup 2% milk

1. Preheat oven to 400°. In a large saucepan, heat butter over medium heat. Add mushrooms, carrots and onion; cook and stir until tender.

2. Stir in flour until blended; gradually stir in broth and milk. Bring to a boil, stirring constantly; cook and stir 2 minutes or until thickened. Stir in chicken, peas, pimientos and salt; heat through. Transfer to a greased 11x7-in. baking dish.

3. For topping, in a large bowl, whisk flour, baking powder, sugar, salt and cream of tartar. Cut in butter until mixture resembles coarse crumbs. Add milk; stir just until moistened.

4. Turn onto a lightly floured surface; knead gently 8-10 times. Pat or roll dough to ½-in. thickness; cut with a floured 2½-in. biscuit cutter. Place over chicken mixture. Bake, uncovered, 15-20 minutes or until biscuits are golden brown.

1 SERVING: 489 cal., 26g fat (14g sat. fat), 118mg chol., 885mg sod., 36g carb. (6g sugars, 3g fiber), 27g pro.

BLUE RIBBON WINNER

JIM'S SECRET FAMILY-RECIPE RIBS

For more than 30 years, my brother-in-law Jim kept his famous rib recipe a secret. When he finally shared it, we just had to pass it along because we loved it so much. This one's for you, Jim!

—*Vicki Young, Brighton, CO*

PREP: 20 MIN. + CHILLING • **COOK:** 3 HOURS 10 MIN. • **MAKES:** 8 SERVINGS

2 racks pork baby back ribs (about 5 lbs.)
¼ cup soy sauce
¼ cup dried oregano
2 Tbsp. onion powder
2 tsp. garlic powder
1 liter lemon-lime soda
½ cup unsweetened pineapple or orange juice, optional

BARBECUE SAUCE
½ cup sugar or packed brown sugar
½ cup hot water
1 cup ketchup
¼ cup honey mustard
¼ cup barbecue sauce of choice
3 Tbsp. lemon juice
1½ tsp. white vinegar

1. Brush ribs with soy sauce. Combine oregano, onion powder and garlic powder; rub over both sides of ribs. Transfer to a large shallow roasting pan; refrigerate, covered, overnight.

2. Preheat oven to 225°. Add lemon-lime soda and, if desired, juice to roasting pan (do not pour over ribs). Bake, covered, until tender, about 3 hours.

3. Meanwhile, make barbecue sauce by dissolving sugar in hot water; combine with remaining ingredients, thinning with additional lemon-lime soda or juice if necessary. Reserve 1 cup for serving.

4. Remove ribs from oven; discard juices. Brush both sides with barbecue sauce. Grill the ribs, covered, on a greased grill rack over low direct heat, turning and brushing occasionally with the remaining sauce, until heated through, about 10 minutes. Cut into serving-size pieces; serve with reserved sauce.

1 SERVING: 483 cal., 27g fat (10g sat. fat), 102mg chol., 1107mg sod., 31g carb. (26g sugars, 1g fiber), 30g pro.

BLUE RIBBON WINNER

CLOCKWISE FROM RIGHT:

COUNTRY OASIS
"This scenic garden means so much to my family, and we all cherish it, each in our own way. This oasis touches the hearts of all who enter."

—*Jolie Raimondo, Waverly, Minnesota*

DAYDREAMER
"My granddaughter Paisley peeks out of the barn, dreaming of adventure."

—*Jacquie Parr, Santa Rosa, California*

PEEK-A-BOO
"One of our newly hatched baby chicks peeks out from under Momma's feathers. It is hard to believe there are nine more underneath her!"

—*Rachel Clelland, Lake Norden, South Dakota*

SUNDOWN SENSATION
"This beloved windmill is a subject I never seem to tire of photographing. The sky behind it is always changing, creating many different moods and scenes, like this vivid sunset."
—*Katherine Plessner, Verona, North Dakota*

BLUE
RIBBON
WINNER

SPICY CHICKEN & BACON MAC

I've been working to perfect a creamy, spicy mac and cheese for years.
After adding smoky bacon, chicken, jalapenos and spicy cheese, this is the ultimate.
—*Sarah Gilbert, Beaverton, OR*

TAKES: 30 MIN. • MAKES: 6 SERVINGS

1½ cups uncooked cavatappi
  pasta or elbow macaroni
3 Tbsp. butter
3 Tbsp. all-purpose flour
1½ cups heavy
  whipping cream
½ cup 2% milk
1 tsp. Cajun seasoning
¼ tsp. salt
¼ tsp. pepper
2 cups shredded
  pepper jack cheese
2 cups shredded
  cooked chicken
6 bacon strips, cooked
  and crumbled
1 jalapeno pepper,
  seeded and chopped
1 cup crushed kettle-
  cooked potato chips or
  panko bread crumbs

1. Cook pasta according to package directions for al dente; drain. Preheat broiler.

2. In a 10-in. cast-iron or other ovenproof skillet, heat butter over medium heat. Stir in flour until blended; cook and stir until lightly browned, 1-2 minutes (do not burn). Gradually whisk in cream, milk, Cajun seasoning, salt and pepper. Bring to a boil, stirring constantly. Reduce heat; cook and stir until thickened, about 5 minutes. Stir in cheese until melted. Add pasta, chicken, bacon and jalapeno; cook and stir until heated through. Sprinkle chips over top.

3. Broil 3-4 in. from heat until the chips are browned, about 30 seconds.

1 CUP: 673 cal., 50g fat (28g sat. fat), 175mg chol., 705mg sod., 26g carb. (3g sugars, 1g fiber), 32g pro.

KITCHEN TIP: If your family likes spicy foods, add more Cajun seasoning or jalapeno pepper.

ROASTED CHICKEN WITH ROSEMARY

Herbs, garlic and butter give this hearty meal in one a classic flavor.
It's a lot like pot roast, only it uses chicken instead of beef.

—Isabel Zienkosky, Salt Lake City, UT

PREP: 20 MIN. • BAKE: 2 HOURS + STANDING • MAKES: 9 SERVINGS

½ cup butter, cubed
4 Tbsp. minced fresh
   rosemary or 2 Tbsp.
   dried rosemary, crushed
2 Tbsp. minced
   fresh parsley
1 tsp. salt
½ tsp. pepper
3 garlic cloves, minced
1 whole roasting
   chicken (5 to 6 lbs.)
6 small red potatoes,
   halved
6 medium carrots,
   halved lengthwise and
   cut into 2-in. pieces
2 medium onions,
   quartered

1. In a small saucepan, melt butter; stir in the seasonings and garlic. Place the chicken breast side up on a rack in a shallow roasting pan; tie drumsticks together with kitchen string. Spoon half of the butter mixture over chicken. Place the potatoes, carrots and onions around chicken. Drizzle remaining butter mixture over vegetables.

2. Bake at 350° for 1½ hours. Baste with cooking juices; bake 30-60 minutes longer, basting occasionally, until a thermometer inserted in thickest part of thigh reads 170°-175°. (Cover loosely with foil if chicken browns too quickly.)

3. Let stand 10-15 minutes, tented with foil if necessary, before carving. Serve with vegetables.

1 SERVING: 449 cal., 28g fat (11g sat. fat), 126mg chol., 479mg sod., 16g carb. (5g sugars, 3g fiber), 33g pro.

SMOKY ESPRESSO STEAK

This juicy steak rubbed with espresso, cocoa and pumpkin pie spice is one of my husband's favorites. We usually grill it, but broiling works just as well.

—Deborah Biggs, Omaha, NE

TAKES: 30 MIN. • **MAKES:** 4 SERVINGS

3 tsp. instant espresso powder
2 tsp. brown sugar
1½ tsp. smoked or regular paprika
1 tsp. salt
1 tsp. baking cocoa
¼ tsp. pumpkin pie spice
¼ tsp. pepper
1 lb. beef flat iron or top sirloin steak (¾ in. thick)

1. Preheat broiler. Mix first 7 ingredients; rub over both sides of steak. Place steak on a broiler pan; let stand 10 minutes.

2. Broil steak 3-4 in. from heat 4-6 minutes on each side or until meat reaches desired doneness (for medium-rare, a thermometer should read 135°; medium, 140°; medium-well, 145°). Let stand 5 minutes before slicing.

3 OZ. COOKED BEEF: 216 cal., 12g fat (5g sat. fat), 73mg chol., 661mg sod., 4g carb. (2g sugars, 0 fiber), 22g pro.

DIABETIC EXCHANGES: 3 lean meat.

BARBECUED PICNIC CHICKEN

I like to serve this savory chicken at family picnics. Cooked on a covered grill, the poultry stays so tender and juicy. Everyone loves the zesty, slightly sweet homemade barbecue sauce—and it's so easy to make.

—Priscilla Weaver, Hagerstown, MD

PREP: 15 MIN. • GRILL: 45 MIN. • MAKES: 8 SERVINGS

2   garlic cloves, minced
2   tsp. butter
1   cup ketchup
¼   cup packed brown sugar
¼   cup chili sauce
2   Tbsp. Worcestershire
     sauce
1   Tbsp. celery seed
1   Tbsp. prepared mustard
½   tsp. salt
2   dashes hot pepper sauce
2   broiler/fryer chickens
     (3½ to 4 lbs. each), cut up

1. In a large saucepan, saute garlic in butter until tender. Add the next 8 ingredients. Bring to a boil, stirring constantly. Remove from the heat; set aside.

2. On a lightly greased grill rack, grill chicken, covered, over medium heat for 30 minutes, turning occasionally. Baste with sauce. Grill 15 minutes longer or until a thermometer reaches 170°, basting and turning several times.

1 PIECE: 296 cal., 14g fat (4g sat. fat), 79mg chol., 761mg sod., 18g carb. (12g sugars, 1g fiber), 25g pro.

KITCHEN TIP: Try this farm-cooking idea if you don't have a basting brush. Tie a few sprigs of rosemary or another hearty herb together with twine, then baste with it.

BLUE
RIBBON
WINNER

SPICY SHRIMP & GRITS

I combined two of my favorite dishes—fajitas and shrimp with cheesy grits—into this one-dish meal. For more heat, use pepper jack cheese instead of a Mexican cheese blend.

—Arlene Erlbach, Morton Grove, IL

TAKES: 30 MIN. • MAKES: 4 SERVINGS

1 lb. uncooked shrimp (16-20 per lb.), peeled and deveined
2 Tbsp. fajita seasoning mix
1 cup quick-cooking grits
4 cups boiling water
1½ cups shredded Mexican cheese blend
3 Tbsp. 2% milk
2 Tbsp. canola oil
3 medium sweet peppers, seeded and cut into 1 in. strips
1 medium sweet onion, cut into 1-in. strips
1 jar (15½ to 16 oz.) medium chunky salsa
¼ cup orange juice
¼ cup plus 1 Tbsp. fresh cilantro leaves, divided

1. Sprinkle shrimp with fajita seasoning; toss to coat. Set aside.

2. Slowly stir the grits into boiling water. Reduce heat to medium; cook, covered, stirring occasionally, until thickened, 5-7 minutes. Remove from heat. Stir in cheese until melted; stir in milk. Keep warm.

3. In a large skillet, heat oil over medium-high heat. Add peppers and onion; cook and stir until tender and pepper edges are slightly charred. Add salsa, orange juice and shrimp. Cook, stirring constantly, until shrimp turn pink, 4-6 minutes. Stir in ¼ cup cilantro. Remove from heat.

4. Spoon grits into serving bowls; top with shrimp mixture. Sprinkle with remaining cilantro.

1 SERVING: 561 cal., 23g fat (8g sat. fat), 176mg chol., 1324mg sod., 55g carb. (12g sugars, 4g fiber), 33g pro.

KITCHEN TIP: This is an ideal introduction to grits for people who may not have had them before. Their creamy, soft texture balances the rest of the ingredients and lets the grits shine.

HORSERADISH-ENCRUSTED BEEF TENDERLOIN

Wow friends and family with this tender beef in a golden horseradish crust. It's perfect for weekend dinners with guests. Roasted garlic boosts the robust flavor even more.

—Laura Bagozzi, Dublin, OH

PREP: 35 MIN. + COOLING • **BAKE:** 45 MIN. + STANDING • **MAKES:** 8 SERVINGS

1   **whole garlic bulb**
1   **tsp. olive oil**
⅓ **cup prepared horseradish**
¼ **tsp. salt**
¼ **tsp. dried basil**
¼ **tsp. dried thyme**
¼ **tsp. pepper**
⅓ **cup soft bread crumbs**
1   **beef tenderloin roast (3 lbs.)**

1. Remove papery outer skin from garlic bulb (do not peel or separate cloves). Cut top off garlic bulb; brush with oil. Wrap in heavy-duty foil. Bake at 425° until softened, 30-35 minutes. Cool for 10-15 minutes.

2. Squeeze softened garlic into a small bowl; stir in horseradish, salt, basil, thyme and pepper. Add bread crumbs; toss to coat. Spread over top of tenderloin. Place on a rack in a large shallow roasting pan.

3. Bake at 400° until the meat reaches desired doneness (for medium-rare, a thermometer should read 135°; medium, 140°; medium-well, 145°), 45-55 minutes. Let stand for 10 minutes before slicing.

5 OZ. COOKED BEEF: 268 cal., 11g fat (4g sat. fat), 75mg chol., 119mg sod., 4g carb. (1g sugars, 1g fiber), 37g pro.

DIABETIC EXCHANGES: 5 lean meat.

MANY HANDS MAKE LIGHT WORK

BY WENDY CHIAPPARO, MENA, ARKANSAS

My garden is my refuge. I have seven children, so our house is often a scene of lively chaos. But my garden always helps me relax and recharge.

Whenever the children followed me into the garden, I handed out chores. "You weed the beans, and you mulch the peppers." Soon they would be hot or tired and would leave me to myself.

One spring, while I was thumbing through seed catalogs, my 9-year-old daughter began cutting pictures from a Burpee catalog. We put our "lists" together and ordered twice as many seeds.

A few days later, while I was preparing the soil, my 13-year-old son picked up a shovel and began helping. We dug up and composted the pea patch lickety-split, and I truly enjoyed his company.

The same thing happened while picking rocks and planting seeds. Each time, one or two of the children wanted to participate. I was surprised to find the work was lighter for their help, and their laughter made the time pass much faster.

As spring became summer, I expected the children to disappear, but no. There they were— watering, pulling weeds and checking for insects.

One day I snuck out to the garden, feeling a little guilty. The sugar snap peas were ripe, and I wanted a taste. As I grazed along the row, a voice piped up behind me, "Whatcha eatin', Mama?"

Abby's big blue eyes sparkled as I showed her how to pop the peas into her mouth. Then my sweet 7-year-old girl put me to shame: "I've got to pick a bunch. I can't wait to share with the others."

I realized how selfish I'd been. I'd tried to keep the joys of gardening to myself, and here was a child who couldn't wait to share. Through tears, I said, "Sure, honey, let's pick a bunch, and I'll show you how to fix them. We'll make a wonderful supper."

Now I share all of the garden's pleasures with the children. We bring the fruits of our labor back home and prepare the produce together, because we know that everything is better when shared.

Opposite page: Abigail, Caleb and Joy Chiapparo (from left) find a summer shower and a rainbow. Top: Hope, Josiah, Wendy and Grace (from left) pinch back basil. Bottom left: A bucket of bounty. Bottom right: Wendy's Summer Garden Stir-Fry, recipe on page 196.

SUMMER GARDEN STIR-FRY

I tend to substitute vegetables in this quick dish depending on what's in season. Sometimes I add baby green beans or whatever else is ready from our garden.

—*Wendy Chiapparo, Mena, AR*

TAKES: 30 MIN. • MAKES: 4 SERVINGS

2 Tbsp. cornstarch
1⅓ cups chicken broth
3 Tbsp. cider vinegar
2 Tbsp. brown sugar
2 Tbsp. soy sauce
¼ tsp. crushed red pepper flakes
2 Tbsp. olive oil, divided
1 lb. boneless skinless chicken breasts, cut into ¾-in. cubes
2 medium carrots, thinly sliced diagonally
1 medium zucchini, halved lengthwise and sliced
1 medium yellow summer squash, halved lengthwise and sliced
1 medium sweet red pepper, julienned
2 garlic cloves, minced
1 tsp. minced fresh gingerroot
6 green onions, sliced diagonally
Hot cooked rice

1. Mix the first 6 ingredients until blended. In a large skillet, heat 1 Tbsp. oil over medium-high heat; stir-fry chicken until no longer pink, 4-5 minutes. Remove from pan.

2. In same pan, heat remaining oil over medium-high heat. Stir-fry carrots, zucchini and yellow squash 2 minutes. Add pepper, garlic and ginger; stir fry until pepper is crisp-tender, 1-2 minutes.

3. Stir cornstarch mixture into vegetables. Bring to a boil; cook and stir until sauce is thickened, 2-3 minutes. Stir in green onions and chicken; heat through. Serve with rice.

1 SERVING: 284 cal., 10g fat (2g sat. fat), 64mg chol., 878mg sod., 21g carb. (12g sugars, 3g fiber), 27g pro.

DIABETIC EXCHANGES: 3 lean meat, 2 fat, 1 starch, 1 vegetable.

MAPLE-PEACH GLAZED HAM

This is one of my husband's all-time favorite recipes. He makes it regularly for his friends on weekends because it's so tasty and so easy to prepare.
—*Bonnie Hawkins, Elkhorn, WI*

PREP: 5 MIN. • **BAKE:** 2 HOURS • **MAKES:** 16 SERVINGS (ABOUT 2 CUPS SAUCE)

1 fully cooked bone-in ham (7 to 9 lbs.)
2 cups peach preserves or orange marmalade
½ cup maple syrup
⅓ cup orange juice
2 Tbsp. ground ancho chili pepper, optional

1. Preheat oven to 325°. Place ham on a rack in a shallow roasting pan. Cover and bake 1¾-2¼ hours or until a thermometer reads 130°.

2. Meanwhile, in a small saucepan, mix the preserves, syrup, orange juice and, if desired, chili pepper until blended. Remove ¾ cup mixture for glaze.

3. Remove ham from oven; brush with some of the glaze. Bake, uncovered, 15-20 minutes longer or until a thermometer reads 140°, brushing occasionally with remaining glaze.

4. In a saucepan over medium heat, bring the preserves mixture to a boil, stirring occasionally. Cook and stir until slightly thickened, 1-2 minutes. Serve as a sauce with ham.

4 OZ. COOKED HAM WITH 2 TBSP. SAUCE: 294 cal., 5g fat (2g sat. fat), 87mg chol., 1040mg sod., 34g carb. (31g sugars, 0 fiber), 29g pro.

BLUE
RIBBON
WINNER

HONEY WALLEYE

Our state is known as the Land of 10,000 Lakes, so fishing is a favorite hobby here. This recipe is my quick way to prepare all the fresh walleye hooked by the anglers in my family.
—*Kitty McCue, St. Louis Park, MN*

TAKES: 20 MIN. • MAKES: 6 SERVINGS

1 large egg
2 tsp. honey
2 cups crushed Ritz crackers (about 45 to 50)
½ tsp. salt
1½ lbs. walleye fillets
⅓ to ½ cup canola oil
   Optional: Minced fresh parsley and lemon wedges

1. In a shallow bowl, beat egg; add honey. In a shallow dish, combine crackers and salt. Dip fish in egg mixture, then in cracker mixture; turn until coated.

2. In a cast-iron or other heavy skillet, cook fillets in oil over medium heat until golden and fish flakes easily with a fork, 3-5 minutes on each side. If desired, top with parsley and serve with lemon wedges.

3 OZ. COOKED FISH: 389 cal., 22g fat (3g sat. fat), 133mg chol., 514mg sod., 23g carb. (5g sugars, 1g fiber), 25g pro.

ITALIAN PASTA BAKE

I love to make this whenever I need to bring a dish to pass. Fresh tomatoes add
a nice touch that seems to be missing from most other meaty casseroles.

—Karla Johnson, East Helena, MT

PREP: 40 MIN. • BAKE: 25 MIN. • MAKES: 8 SERVINGS

2 lbs. ground beef
1 large onion, chopped
2 garlic cloves, minced
1 jar (24 oz.)
  spaghetti sauce
1 can (14½ oz.) diced
  tomatoes, undrained
1 can (4 oz.) mushroom
  stems and pieces,
  drained
1 tsp. Italian seasoning
3 cups uncooked
  medium pasta shells
3 plum tomatoes, sliced
¾ cup shredded
  provolone cheese
¾ cup shredded part-skim
  mozzarella cheese

1. In a large skillet, cook beef and onion over medium heat until no longer pink. Add garlic; cook 1 minute longer. Drain. Stir in the spaghetti sauce, diced tomatoes, mushrooms and Italian seasoning. Bring to a boil. Reduce heat; simmer, uncovered, 20 minutes.

2. Meanwhile, preheat oven to 350°. Cook pasta according to package directions; drain. Add to beef mixture and gently stir in the sliced plum tomatoes.

3. Transfer to an ungreased 13x9-in. baking dish. Sprinkle with the cheeses. Bake 25-30 minutes or until bubbly and heated through.

1½ CUPS: 489 cal., 20g fat (8g sat. fat), 80mg chol., 702mg sod., 45g carb. (10g sugars, 5g fiber), 32g pro.

KITCHEN TIP: Before adding vegetables to a casserole, it's best to cook them first. Be sure to strain out any excess liquid from the cooking process. Not doing so may make the final dish watery.

TENDER SWEET & SOUR PORK CHOPS

My best friend gave me the recipe for these delightful pork chops years ago.
It's become one of my family's most-requested dinners, so I prepare it often.

—*Gina Young, Lamar, CO*

TAKES: 25 MIN. • MAKES: 6 SERVINGS

6   boneless pork loin
    chops (4 oz. each)
¾   tsp. pepper
½   cup water
⅓   cup cider vinegar
¼   cup packed brown sugar
2   Tbsp. reduced-sodium
    soy sauce
1   Tbsp. Worcestershire
    sauce
1   Tbsp. cornstarch
2   Tbsp. cold water

1. Sprinkle pork chops with pepper. In a large skillet coated with cooking spray, cook pork over medium heat for 4-6 minutes on each side or until lightly browned. Remove and keep warm.

2. Add the water, vinegar, brown sugar, soy sauce and Worcestershire sauce to skillet; stir to loosen browned bits. Bring to a boil. Combine cornstarch and cold water until smooth; stir into skillet. Bring to a boil; cook and stir for 2 minutes or until thickened.

3. Return chops to the pan. Reduce heat; cover and simmer for 4-5 minutes or until meat is tender.

1 PORK CHOP WITH 3 TBSP. SAUCE: 198 cal., 6g fat (2g sat. fat), 55mg chol., 265mg sod., 12g carb. (10g sugars, 0 fiber), 22g pro.

DIABETIC EXCHANGES: 3 lean meat, 1 starch.

SLOPPY JOE UNDER A BUN

I usually keep a can of sloppy joe sauce in the pantry because our kids love sloppy joes. But I don't always have buns on hand. With this fun casserole, we can enjoy the flavor they adore anytime.

—*Trish Bloom, Ray, MI*

PREP: 15 MIN. • **BAKE:** 25 MIN. • **MAKES:** 8 SERVINGS

1½ lbs. ground beef
1 can (15½ oz.) sloppy
    joe sauce
2 cups shredded
    cheddar cheese
2 cups biscuit/baking mix
2 large eggs, lightly beaten
1 cup 2% milk
1 Tbsp. sesame seeds

1. In a large skillet, cook beef over medium heat until no longer pink; drain. Stir in sloppy joe sauce. Transfer to a lightly greased 13x9-in. baking dish; sprinkle with cheese.

2. In a large bowl, combine the biscuit mix, eggs and milk just until blended. Pour over cheese; sprinkle with sesame seeds. Bake, uncovered, at 400° for 25 minutes or until golden brown.

1 SERVING: 423 cal., 23g fat (12g sat. fat), 129mg chol., 961mg sod., 26g carb. (6g sugars, 1g fiber), 27g pro.

BLUE RIBBON WINNER

OVEN-FRIED CHICKEN DRUMSTICKS

This fabulous recipe uses Greek yogurt to create an amazing marinade that makes the chicken incredibly moist. No one will guess that it has been lightened up and is not actually fried!

—*Kimberly Wallace, Dennison, OH*

PREP: 20 MIN. + MARINATING • **BAKE:** 40 MIN. • **MAKES:** 4 SERVINGS

- 1 cup fat-free plain Greek yogurt
- 1 Tbsp. Dijon mustard
- 2 garlic cloves, minced
- 8 chicken drumsticks (4 oz. each), skin removed
- ½ cup whole wheat flour
- 1½ tsp. paprika
- 1 tsp. baking powder
- 1 tsp. salt
- 1 tsp. pepper
  Olive oil-flavored cooking spray

1. In a large bowl or dish, combine yogurt, mustard and garlic. Add chicken and turn to coat. Cover and refrigerate 8 hours or overnight.

2. Preheat oven to 425°. In another bowl, mix flour, paprika, baking powder, salt and pepper. Remove chicken from the marinade and add, 1 piece at a time, to flour mixture; toss to coat. Place on a wire rack over a baking sheet; spritz with cooking spray. Bake 40-45 minutes or until a thermometer reads 170°-175°.

2 CHICKEN DRUMSTICKS: 227 cal., 7g fat (1g sat. fat), 81mg chol., 498mg sod., 9g carb. (2g sugars, 1g fiber), 31g pro.

DIABETIC EXCHANGES: 4 lean meat, ½ starch.

KITCHEN TIP: To prepare in an air fryer, preheat air fryer to 375°. In batches, arrange coated chicken in a single layer on greased tray in air-fryer basket. Cook until a thermometer reads 170°, turning halfway, about 20 minutes total. Repeat with remaining chicken. When the last batch of chicken is cooked, return all chicken to basket and cook 2-3 minutes longer to heat through.

BLEND OF THE BAYOU

My sister-in-law shared this recipe with me when I first moved to Louisiana. It's been handed down in my husband's family for generations. I've passed it on to our children, too.

—Ruby Williams, Bogalusa, LA

PREP: 20 MIN. • BAKE: 25 MIN. • MAKES: 8 SERVINGS

1 pkg. (8 oz.) cream cheese, cubed
4 Tbsp. butter, divided
1 large onion, chopped
2 celery ribs, chopped
1 large green pepper, chopped
1 lb. cooked medium shrimp, peeled and deveined
2 cans (6 oz. each) crabmeat, drained, flaked and cartilage removed
1 can (10¾ oz.) condensed cream of mushroom soup, undiluted
¾ cup cooked rice
1 jar (4½ oz.) sliced mushrooms, drained
1 tsp. garlic salt
¾ tsp. hot pepper sauce
½ tsp. cayenne pepper
¾ cup shredded cheddar cheese
½ cup crushed butter-flavored crackers (about 12 crackers)

1. Preheat oven to 350°. In a small saucepan, cook and stir cream cheese and 2 Tbsp. butter over low heat until melted and smooth.

2. In a large cast-iron or other ovenproof skillet, saute the onion, celery and green pepper in remaining butter until tender. Stir in shrimp, crab, soup, rice, mushrooms, garlic salt, pepper sauce, cayenne and cream cheese mixture.

3. Combine cheddar cheese and cracker crumbs; sprinkle over top. Bake, uncovered, until bubbly, 25-30 minutes.

1 CUP: 366 cal., 23g fat (13g sat. fat), 164mg chol., 981mg sod., 17g carb. (3g sugars, 2g fiber), 23g pro.

LONG DAY'S REWARD
"After a long judging event, Becky and her friend Daffodil slept quietly in the straw."
—Sandy Kline,
New Haven, Connecticut

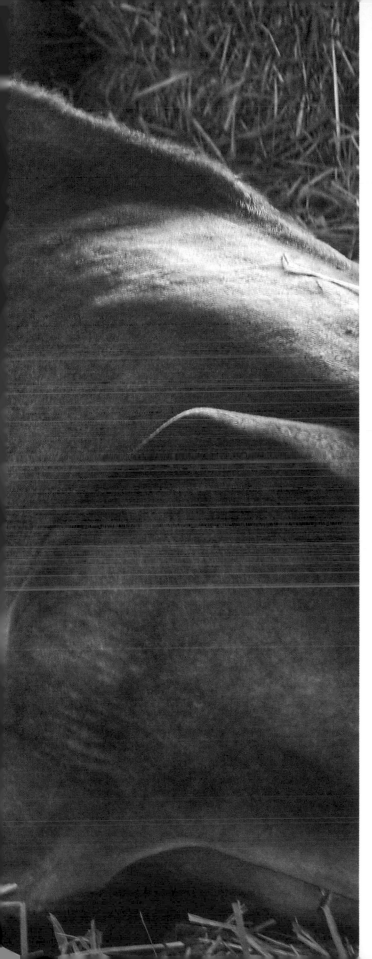

FROM TOP:

SENTIMENTAL JOURNEY
"This International Harvester tractor has been in our family for years. I snapped this picture just as the sun began to set."

—*Rebecca Finchum, Strawberry Plains, Tennessee*

KIDS THESE DAYS
"I liked the sweet way this kid was standing with her mom. We named her Noel because she was born around Christmas."

—*Tanja Hupp, Mount Crawford, Virginia*

ASPARAGUS HAM DINNER

I've been making this light meal for my family for years now, and it's always well received. With asparagus, tomato, pasta and ham, it's a tempting blend of tastes and textures.
—*Rhonda Zavodny, David City, NE*

TAKES: 25 MIN. • MAKES: 6 SERVINGS

2 cups uncooked corkscrew or spiral pasta
¾ lb. fresh asparagus, cut into 1-in. pieces
1 medium sweet yellow pepper, julienned
1 Tbsp. olive oil
6 medium tomatoes, diced
6 oz. boneless fully cooked ham, cubed
¼ cup minced fresh parsley
½ tsp. salt
½ tsp. dried oregano
½ tsp. dried basil
⅛ to ¼ tsp. cayenne pepper
¼ cup shredded Parmesan cheese

Cook pasta according to package directions. Meanwhile, in a large cast-iron or other heavy skillet, saute asparagus and yellow pepper in oil until crisp-tender. Add tomatoes and ham; heat through. Drain pasta; add to mixture. Stir in parsley and seasonings. Sprinkle with cheese.

1⅓ CUPS: 204 cal., 5g fat (1g sat. fat), 17mg chol., 561mg sod., 29g carb. (5g sugars, 3g fiber), 12g pro.

DIABETIC EXCHANGES: 1½ starch, 1 lean meat, 1 vegetable, ½ fat.

SAGE-RUBBED SALMON

If you've always thought of sage with turkey, try it with salmon for a little taste of heaven.
I like to serve this with rice, salad and sauteed green beans.

—Nicole Raskopf, Beacon, NY

TAKES: 20 MIN. • MAKES: 6 SERVINGS

2 Tbsp. minced fresh sage
1 tsp. garlic powder
1 tsp. kosher salt
1 tsp. freshly
   ground pepper
1 skin-on salmon
   fillet (1½ lbs.)
2 Tbsp. olive oil

1. Preheat oven to 375°. Mix first 4 ingredients; rub onto flesh side of salmon. Cut into 6 portions.

2. In a large cast-iron skillet, heat oil over medium heat. Add salmon, skin side down; cook 5 minutes. Transfer skillet to oven; bake just until fish flakes easily with a fork, about 10 minutes.

3 OZ. COOKED FISH: 220 cal., 1bg fat (3g sat. fat), 57mg chol., 377mg sod., 1g carb. (0 sugars, 0 fiber), 19g pro.

DIABETIC EXCHANGES: 3 lean meat.

FESTIVE MEAT LOAF PINWHEEL

Why not jazz up meat loaf for a special dinner? This crowd-sized entree features ham,
Swiss cheese and an absolutely wonderful homemade tomato sauce.

—Vera Sullivan, Amity, OR

PREP: 20 MIN. • BAKE: 1¼ HOURS • MAKES: 20 SERVINGS

3 **large eggs**
1 **cup dry bread crumbs**
½ **cup finely chopped onion**
½ **cup finely chopped
   green pepper**
¼ **cup ketchup**
2 **tsp. minced fresh parsley**
1 **tsp. dried basil**
1 **tsp. dried oregano**
1 **garlic clove, minced**
2 **tsp. salt**
½ **tsp. pepper**
5 **lbs. lean ground
   beef (90% lean)**
¾ **lb. thinly sliced deli ham**
¾ **lb. thinly sliced
   Swiss cheese**

TOMATO PEPPER SAUCE
½ **cup finely chopped onion**
2 **celery ribs, chopped**
½ **cup chopped
   green pepper**
1 **garlic clove, minced**
1 **to 2 tsp. olive oil**
2 **cups chopped
   fresh tomatoes**
1 **cup beef broth**
1 **bay leaf**
1 **tsp. sugar**
¼ **tsp. salt**
¼ **tsp. dried thyme**
1 **Tbsp. cornstarch**
2 **Tbsp. cold water**

1. In a large bowl, combine the first 11 ingredients. Crumble beef over mixture and mix lightly but thoroughly. On a piece of heavy-duty foil, pat beef mixture into a 17x15-in. rectangle. Cover with ham and cheese slices to within ½ in. of edges.

2. Roll up tightly jelly-roll style, starting with a short side. Place seam side down in a roasting pan. Bake, uncovered, at 350° until a thermometer reads 160°, 1¼-1½ hours.

3. In a large saucepan, saute the onion, celery, green pepper and garlic in oil until tender, 3-5 minutes. Add tomatoes, broth, bay leaf, sugar, salt and thyme. Simmer, uncovered, for 30 minutes. Discard bay leaf.

4. Combine cornstarch and water until smooth; stir into sauce. Bring to a boil; cook and stir until thickened, about 2 minutes. Drain meat loaf. Serve with sauce.

1 SLICE: 319 cal., 17g fat (7g sat. fat), 124mg chol., 732mg sod., 8g carb. (2g sugars, 1g fiber), 32g pro.

THE BEST BEEF STEW

This stew recipe has tons of flavor, thanks to its blend of herbs and the addition of red wine and balsamic vinegar. It's a comfort classic stepped up a notch.

—James Schend, Pleasant Prairie, WI

PREP: 30 MIN. • COOK: 2 HOURS • MAKES: 6 SERVINGS (2¼ QT.)

1½ lbs. beef stew meat,
   cut into 1-in. cubes
½ tsp. salt, divided
6 Tbsp. all-purpose
   flour, divided
½ tsp. smoked paprika
1 Tbsp. canola oil
3 Tbsp. tomato paste
2 tsp. herbes de Provence
2 garlic cloves, minced
2 cups dry red wine
2 cups beef broth
1½ tsp. minced fresh
   rosemary, divided
2 bay leaves
3 cups cubed peeled
   potatoes
3 cups coarsely chopped
   onions (about 2 large)
2 cups sliced carrots
2 Tbsp. cold water
2 Tbsp. balsamic or
   red wine vinegar
1 cup fresh or frozen peas
   Additional fresh
   rosemary, optional

1. In a small bowl, toss beef and ¼ tsp. salt. In a large bowl, combine 4 Tbsp. flour and paprika. Add beef, a few pieces at a time, and toss to coat.

2. In a Dutch oven, brown beef in oil over medium heat. Stir in tomato paste, herbes de Provence and garlic; cook until fragrant and color starts to darken slightly. Add wine; cook until mixture just comes to a boil. Simmer until reduced by half, about 5 minutes. Stir in broth, 1 tsp. rosemary and bay leaves. Bring to a boil. Reduce heat; cover and simmer until meat is almost tender, about 1½ hours.

3. Add potatoes, onions and carrots. Cover; simmer until meat and vegetables are tender, about 30 minutes longer.

4. Discard bay leaves. In a small bowl, combine remaining ½ tsp. rosemary, remaining ¼ tsp. salt and remaining 2 Tbsp. flour. Add cold water and vinegar; stir until smooth. Stir into stew. Bring to a boil; add peas. Cook, stirring, until thickened, about 2 minutes. If desired, top with additional fresh rosemary.

1½ CUPS: 366 cal., 11g fat (3g sat. fat), 71mg chol., 605mg sod., 40g carb. (9g sugars, 6g fiber), 28g pro.

DIABETIC EXCHANGES: 3 lean meat, 2½ starch, ½ fat.

KITCHEN TIP: Try using chuck, also known as front shoulder meat, for this beef stew. The round, or rear muscle, also works well. While these tough cuts take time to become tender, they release collagen as they cook for a smooth, rich broth.

CHAPTER 7

SLOW COOKER, INSTANT POT® & AIR FRYER

Even when life gets too busy to cook, you can still serve hearty farmhouse favorites. Slow cookers, electric pressure cookers and air fryers quickly turn garden greats into savory comforts.

EVERYTHING-BAGEL CHICKEN STRIPS

I love the flavor profile of everything bagels, so I re-created it with breaded chicken fingers made in an air fryer. Serve them with your favorite dipping sauce.

—*Cyndy Gerken, Naples, FL*

PREP: 10 MIN. • COOK: 15 MIN./BATCH • MAKES: 4 SERVINGS

1   **day-old everything bagel, torn**
½   **cup panko bread crumbs**
½   **cup grated Parmesan cheese**
¼   **tsp. crushed red pepper flakes**
¼   **cup butter, cubed**
1   **lb. chicken tenderloins**
½   **tsp. salt**

1. Preheat air fryer to 400°. Pulse torn bagel in a food processor until coarse crumbs form. Place ½ cup bagel crumbs in a shallow bowl; toss with panko, cheese and pepper flakes. (Discard or save remaining bagel crumbs for another use.)

2. In a microwave-safe shallow bowl, microwave butter until melted. Sprinkle chicken with salt. Dip in warm butter, then coat with crumb mixture, patting to help adhere. In batches, place chicken in a single layer on greased tray in air-fryer basket.

3. Cook 7 minutes; turn chicken. Continue cooking until coating is golden brown and chicken is no longer pink, 7-8 minutes. Serve immediately.

1 SERVING: 269 cal., 13g fat (7g sat. fat), 88mg chol., 663mg sod., 8g carb. (1g sugars, 0 fiber), 31g pro.

KITCHEN TIP: In our testing, we have found cook times vary dramatically between brands of air fryers. As a result, we have given wider than normal ranges on suggested cook times. Begin checking at the first time listed and adjust as needed.

MOIST CORN SPOON BREAD

Enjoy this easy take on a southern specialty by using your slow cooker.
It's an excellent side dish for holidays and special feasts.

—Taste of Home *Test Kitchen*

PREP: 20 MIN. • **COOK:** 4 HOURS • **MAKES:** 8 SERVINGS

1 pkg. (8 oz.) cream
   cheese, softened
2 Tbsp. sugar
2 large eggs, beaten
1 cup 2% milk
2 Tbsp. butter, melted
½ tsp. salt
¼ tsp. cayenne pepper
⅛ tsp. pepper
2 cups frozen corn
1 can (14¾ oz.) cream-
   style corn
1 cup yellow cornmeal
1 cup shredded Monterey
   Jack cheese
3 green onions,
   thinly sliced
   Optional: Coarsely
   ground pepper and thinly
   sliced green onions

1. In a large bowl, beat cream cheese and sugar until smooth. Gradually beat in eggs. Beat in the milk, butter, salt, cayenne and pepper until blended. Stir in the remaining ingredients.

2. Pour into a greased 3-qt. slow cooker. Cover and cook on low for 4-5 hours or until a toothpick inserted in the center comes out clean. If desired, top with the additional pepper and the green onions.

1 SERVING: 350 cal., 18g fat (11g sat. fat), 54mg chol., 525mg sod., 38g carb. (8g sugars, 3g fiber), 12g pro.

RASPBERRY BALSAMIC SMOKED PORK CHOPS

Air-fryer pork chops are so delicious and so easy to make. They're perfect for busy weeknights.
My husband just loves them. The dipping sauce makes the pork seem special.

—Lynn Moretti, Oconomowoc, WI

PREP: 15 MIN. • **COOK:** 15 MIN./BATCH • **MAKES:** 4 SERVINGS

2 large eggs
¼ cup 2% milk
1 cup panko bread crumbs
1 cup finely chopped
   pecans
4 smoked bone-in pork
   chops (7½ oz. each)
¼ cup all-purpose flour
   Cooking spray
⅓ cup balsamic vinegar
2 Tbsp. brown sugar
2 Tbsp. seedless
   raspberry jam
1 Tbsp. thawed frozen
   orange juice concentrate

1. Preheat air fryer to 400°. In a shallow bowl, whisk together the eggs and milk. In another shallow bowl, toss bread crumbs with pecans.

2. Coat pork chops with flour; shake off excess. Dip in egg mixture, then in crumb mixture, patting to help adhere. In batches, place chops in single layer on greased tray in the air-fryer basket; spritz with cooking spray.

3. Cook until golden brown, 12-15 minutes, turning halfway through cooking and spritzing with additional cooking spray. Meanwhile, place the remaining ingredients in a saucepan; bring to a boil. Cook and stir until mixture is slightly thickened, 6-8 minutes. Serve with chops.

NOTE: Cook times vary dramatically between brands of air fryers. Begin checking at the first time listed and adjust as needed.

1 PORK CHOP WITH 1 TBSP. GLAZE: 579 cal., 36g fat (10g sat. fat), 106mg chol., 1374mg sod., 36g carb. (22g sugars, 3g fiber), 32g pro.

SLOW-COOKED BEANS

This flavorful dish adds nice variety to any buffet because it's a bit different than traditional baked beans. It's a snap to prepare, too, since it uses convenient canned beans, barbecue sauce and salsa.

—*Joy Beck, Cincinnati, OH*

PREP: 10 MIN. • **COOK:** 2 HOURS • **MAKES:** 16 SERVINGS

4 cans (15½ oz. each)
   great northern beans,
   rinsed and drained
4 cans (15 oz. each)
   black beans, rinsed
   and drained
2 cans (15 oz. each)
   butter beans, rinsed
   and drained
2¼ cups barbecue sauce
2¼ cups salsa
¾ cup packed brown sugar
½ to 1 tsp. hot pepper sauce

In a 6-qt. slow cooker, gently combine all ingredients. Cook, covered, on low until heated through, about 2 hours.

1 SERVING: 134 cal., 1g fat (0 sat. fat), 0 chol., 657mg sod., 27g carb. (16g sugars, 5g fiber), 4g pro.

SPICY HONEY SRIRACHA GAME DAY DIP

I love slow-cooked dips for parties—just turn the slow cooker to low once it is cooked and let your guests help themselves. No need to worry about the dip getting cold and having to reheat it.

—Julie Peterson, Crofton, MD

PREP: 20 MIN. • COOK: 3 HOURS • MAKES: 3 CUPS

1 lb. ground chicken
1 pkg. (8 oz.) cream cheese, cubed
1 cup shredded white cheddar cheese
¼ cup chicken broth
2 to 4 Tbsp. Sriracha chili sauce
2 Tbsp. honey
    Tortilla chips
    Chopped green onions, optional

1. In a large skillet, cook chicken over medium heat until no longer pink, 6-8 minutes, breaking into crumbles; drain. Transfer to a greased 3-qt. slow cooker. Stir in cream cheese, cheddar cheese, broth, chili sauce and honey.

2. Cook, covered, on low until cheese is melted, 3-4 hours, stirring every 30 minutes. Serve with tortilla chips. If desired, sprinkle with green onions.

¼ CUP: 168 cal., 13g fat (6g sat. fat), 54mg chol., 243mg sod., 5g carb. (4g sugars, 0 fiber), 9g pro.

SLOW & EASY
"I like to imagine that someone out for a bike ride stopped to enjoy the beautiful flowers."
—*Annette Archuleta, Friendswood, Texas*

FROM TOP:

TRUE BLUE
"One day, my fiancee, Brittany, and I took our dog to play in a field of bluebonnets. It's a tradition here in Texas; it just wouldn't be spring without seeing a bluebonnet patch. And Minnie had so much fun!"

—*Daniel Andrade, Hitchcock, Texas*

WARM WELCOME
"When all the baby animals arrive, it's such a joy to watch the children react to them. With a crown of flowers on her head, my niece gave these chicks a warm spring welcome."

—*Lorianne Ende, Rogers, Minnesota*

CAJUN CHICKEN ALFREDO

This one-pot recipe is a true comfort food! Cajun spice adds a heat to the creamy Alfredo sauce. This quick recipe would also be tasty with shrimp or smoked sausage.

—Jennifer Stowell, Deep River, IA

TAKES: 30 MIN. • **MAKES:** 6 SERVINGS

2 Tbsp. olive oil, divided
2 medium green peppers, chopped
2 boneless skinless chicken breasts (6 oz. each), cubed
2 Tbsp. Cajun seasoning, divided
1 pkg. (16 oz.) bow tie pasta
3 cups chicken stock
2 cups water
2 cups heavy whipping cream
1 cup shredded Parmesan cheese

1. Select saute setting on a 6-qt. electric pressure cooker and adjust for medium heat; add 1 Tbsp. oil. When oil is hot, cook and stir peppers until crisp-tender, 3-4 minutes. Remove and keep warm. Heat remaining 1 Tbsp. oil. Add chicken and 1 Tbsp. Cajun seasoning. Cook and stir until browned, 3-4 minutes. Press cancel.

2. Add the pasta, stock and water (do not stir). Lock lid; close pressure-release valve. Adjust to pressure-cook on high for 6 minutes. Let pressure release naturally for 3 minutes; quick-release any remaining pressure.

3. Select saute setting, and adjust for low heat. Stir in cream, Parmesan cheese, remaining 1 Tbsp. Cajun seasoning and cooked peppers. Cook until heated through (do not boil).

1⅔ CUPS: 717 cal., 40g fat (22g sat. fat), 131mg chol., 935mg sod., 60g carb. (6g sugars, 3g fiber), 31g pro.

BLUE
RIBBON
WINNER

GARLIC-ROSEMARY BRUSSELS SPROUTS

This is my go-to air-fried side dish. It's healthy, easy and doesn't take very much time or effort to make. It's wonderful alongside turkey that's been seasoned with herbs.

—*Elisabeth Larsen, Pleasant Grove, UT*

TAKES: 30 MIN. • MAKES: 4 SERVINGS

3 Tbsp. olive oil
2 garlic cloves, minced
½ tsp. salt
¼ tsp. pepper
1 lb. Brussels sprouts, trimmed and halved
½ cup panko bread crumbs
1½ tsp. minced fresh rosemary

1. Preheat air fryer to 350°. Place first 4 ingredients in a small microwave-safe bowl; microwave on high 30 seconds.

2. Toss Brussels sprouts with 2 Tbsp. oil mixture. Place Brussels sprouts on tray in air-fryer basket; cook 4-5 minutes. Stir sprouts. Cook until sprouts are lightly browned and near desired tenderness, about 8 minutes longer, stirring halfway through cooking time.

Toss bread crumbs with rosemary and remaining oil mixture; sprinkle over sprouts. Continue cooking until the crumbs are browned and sprouts are tender, 3-5 minutes. Serve the sprouts immediately.

NOTE: Cook times vary dramatically between brands of air fryers. Begin checking at the first time listed and adjust as needed.

¾ **CUP:** 164 cal., 11g fat (1g sat. fat), 0 chol., 342mg sod., 15g carb. (3g sugars, 4g fiber), 5g pro.

DIABETIC EXCHANGES: 2 fat, 1 vegetable, ½ starch.

STUFFED CHICKEN ROLLS

Just thinking about this dish sparks my appetite. The ham and cheese rolled inside are a tasty surprise. Leftovers reheat well and make a perfect lunch with green salad.

—Jean Sherwood, Kenneth City, FL

PREP: 25 MIN. + CHILLING • COOK: 4 HOURS • MAKES: 6 SERVINGS

6 boneless skinless
   chicken breast
   halves (8 oz. each)
6 slices fully cooked ham
6 slices Swiss cheese
¼ cup all-purpose flour
¼ cup grated Parmesan
   cheese
½ tsp. rubbed sage
¼ tsp. paprika
¼ tsp. pepper
¼ cup canola oil
1 can (10¾ oz.) condensed
   cream of chicken
   soup, undiluted
½ cup chicken broth
   Chopped fresh parsley,
   optional

1. Flatten chicken to ¼-in. thickness; top with ham and cheese. Roll up and tuck in ends; secure with toothpicks.

2. In a shallow bowl, combine the flour, cheese, sage, paprika and pepper; coat chicken on all sides. In a large skillet, brown chicken in oil over medium-high heat.

3. Transfer to a 5-qt. slow cooker. Combine soup and broth; pour over the chicken. Cover and cook on low for 4-5 hours or until chicken is tender. Remove the toothpicks. Garnish with parsley if desired.

FREEZE OPTION: Cool chicken mixture. Freeze in freezer containers. To use, partially thaw in refrigerator overnight. Heat through slowly in a covered skillet, stirring occasionally, until a thermometer inserted in chicken reads 165°.

1 STUFFED CHICKEN BREAST HALF: 525 cal., 26g fat (10g sat. fat), 167mg chol., 914mg sod., 9g carb. (1g sugars, 1g fiber), 60g pro.

BLUE
RIBBON
WINNER

AIR-FRIED APPLE-PIE ROLLS

Whip up these easy treats whenever you get a craving for apple pie. The air fryer turns egg roll wrappers into crispy, crunchy crusts without all the work. We love the tender, juicy filling as well.

—Sheila Suhan, Scottdale, PA

PREP: 25 MIN. • COOK: 15 MIN./BATCH • MAKES: 8 SERVINGS

3 cups chopped peeled
  tart apples
½ cup packed light
  brown sugar
2½ tsp. ground
  cinnamon, divided
1 tsp. cornstarch
8 egg roll wrappers
½ cup spreadable
  cream cheese
  Butter-flavored cooking
  spray
1 Tbsp. sugar
⅔ cup hot caramel ice
  cream topping

1. Preheat air fryer to 400°. In a small bowl, combine apples, brown sugar, 2 tsp. cinnamon and cornstarch. With a corner of an egg roll wrapper facing you, spread 1 scant Tbsp. cream cheese to within 1 in. of edges. Place ⅓ cup apple mixture just below center of wrapper. (Cover remaining wrappers with a damp paper towel until ready to use.)

2. Fold bottom corner over filling; moisten remaining wrapper edges with water. Fold side corners toward center over filling. Roll egg roll up tightly, pressing at tip to seal. Repeat.

3. In batches, arrange egg rolls in a single layer on greased tray in air-fryer basket; spritz with cooking spray. Cook until golden brown, 5-6 minutes. Turn; spritz with cooking spray. Cook until golden brown and crisp, 5-6 minutes longer. Combine sugar and remaining ½ tsp. cinnamon; carefully roll hot egg rolls in mixture. Serve with caramel sauce.

NOTE: Cook times vary dramatically between brands of air fryers. Begin checking at the first time listed and adjust as needed.

1 ROLL: 273 cal., 4g fat (2g sat. fat), 13mg chol., 343mg sod., 56g carb. (35g sugars, 2g fiber), 5g pro.

A CENTURY AND STILL GROWING

STORY BY MEGHAN HIHN KLOTZBACH AND MATT HIHN
WEST GROVE, PENNSYLVANIA

My brother, Matt Hihn, and I are the fifth generation of ownership at C.P. Yeatman & Sons Inc. and Mother Earth Organic Mushrooms. (C.P. Yeatman was our great-grandfather.) The Yeatmans purchased the family farm in 1919, and our ancestors built their first mushroom house on the original dairy farm in 1921.

Since then, our mushroom production has grown to nearly 17 million pounds per year. We converted to organic in '89, the first commercial mushroom farm in the United States to do so. Today, all of our mushrooms are certified organic.

Matt and I got into the business in different ways. My brother wanted to be a mushroom farmer since he was little. He started working here part time while he was in high school and full time after finishing college.

I earned a degree in psychology. Initially I had no interest in going into the family business, but after working elsewhere, coupled with lengthy conversations with Matt, our dad and my husband (who also works on the farm), I decided working with my family could be very rewarding.

I began by learning all about occupational and food safety requirements, how to build and implement programs, and the organic certification process. I am currently the VP of operations, sales and marketing in our packaging and sales division.

One of the perks of my job is giving tours. Our work seems normal to me, but seeing visitors' eyes light up reminds me how special it really is.

Dad plans on retiring in about five years, but for now we enjoy working alongside one another. We work well together and hope our business thrives for our children and many generations to come.

PHOTOS BY JIM COARSE, MOONLOOP PHOTOGRAPHY

Left: Siblings Meghan and Matt pause while inspecting growing beds.
Top: The Hihns grow white, portobello and cremini mushrooms at their facilities in Oxford (pictured) and West Grove.
Bottom: Mushrooms are sliced for packaging.

CONTEST-WINNING MUSHROOM POT ROAST

Packed with wholesome veggies and tender beef, this sure is one company-special entree...even though it comes from a slow cooker. Serve mashed potatoes on the side to soak up the beefy gravy.

—Angie Stewart, Topeka, KS

PREP: 25 MIN. • COOK: 6 HOURS • MAKES: 10 SERVINGS

1 boneless beef chuck roast (3 to 4 lbs.)
½ tsp. salt
¼ tsp. pepper
1 Tbsp. canola oil
1½ lbs. sliced fresh shiitake mushrooms
2½ cups thinly sliced onions
1½ cups reduced-sodium beef broth
1½ cups dry red wine or additional reduced-sodium beef broth
1 can (8 oz.) tomato sauce
¾ cup chopped peeled parsnips
¾ cup chopped celery
¾ cup chopped carrots
8 garlic cloves, minced
2 bay leaves
1½ tsp. dried thyme
1 tsp. chili powder
¼ cup cornstarch
¼ cup water
   Mashed potatoes

1. Sprinkle roast with salt and pepper. In a Dutch oven, brown roast in oil on all sides. Transfer to a 6-qt. slow cooker. Add the mushrooms, onions, broth, wine, tomato sauce, parsnips, celery, carrots, garlic, bay leaves, thyme and chili powder. Cover and cook on low for 6-8 hours or until meat is tender.

2. Remove meat and vegetables to a serving platter; keep warm. Discard bay leaves. Skim fat from cooking juices; transfer to a small saucepan. Bring liquid to a boil. Combine cornstarch and water until smooth; gradually stir into the pan. Bring to a boil; cook and stir for 2 minutes or until thickened. Serve with mashed potatoes, meat and vegetables.

4 OZ. COOKED BEEF WITH ⅔ CUP VEGETABLES AND ½ CUP GRAVY: 310 cal., 14g fat (5g sat. fat), 89mg chol., 363mg sod., 14g carb. (4g sugars, 3g fiber), 30g pro.

DIABETIC EXCHANGES: 4 lean meat, 2 vegetable, 1½ fat.

BLUE RIBBON WINNER

CRAZY DELICIOUS BABY BACK RIBS

My husband often craves baby back ribs, so we cook them multiple ways.
This low and slow method creates a tangy sauce that's the best we've found.

—Jan Whitworth, Roebuck, SC

PREP: 15 MIN. • COOK: 5¼ HOURS • MAKES: 8 SERVINGS

2 Tbsp. smoked paprika
2 tsp. chili powder
2 tsp. garlic salt
1 tsp. onion powder
1 tsp. pepper
½ tsp. cayenne pepper
4 lbs. pork baby back ribs

SAUCE
½ cup Worcestershire
   sauce
½ cup mayonnaise
½ cup yellow mustard
¼ cup reduced-sodium
   soy sauce
3 Tbsp. hot pepper sauce

1. In a small bowl, combine the first 6 ingredients. Cut ribs into serving-size pieces; rub with seasoning mixture. Place ribs in a 6-qt. slow cooker. Cook, covered, on low until meat is tender, 5-6 hours.

2. Preheat oven to 375°. In a small bowl, whisk the sauce ingredients. Transfer ribs to a foil-lined 15x10x1-in. baking pan; brush with some of the sauce. Bake 15-20 minutes or until browned, turning once and brushing occasionally with sauce. Serve with remaining sauce.

1 SERVING: 420 cal., 33g fat (9g sat. fat), 86mg chol., 1082mg sod., 6g carb. (2g sugars, 2g fiber), 24g pro.

SLOW-COOKER JAMBALAYA RISOTTO

I love risotto, but I don't love all the stirring it takes to create its signature creamy goodness.
I found a slow-cooker risotto recipe and adapted it to a jambalaya recipe for this dish.

—Angela Westra, Cambridge, MA

PREP: 20 MIN. • COOK: 2 HOURS • MAKES: 6 SERVINGS

2½ cups chicken broth
1 can (14½ oz.) diced
  tomatoes, undrained
1½ cups tomato sauce
1¼ cups uncooked
  arborio rice
3 Tbsp. finely
  chopped onion
1 Tbsp. dried
  parsley flakes
1 Tbsp. olive oil
½ tsp. garlic powder
½ tsp. dried thyme
½ tsp. pepper
¼ tsp. salt
¼ tsp. cayenne pepper
1 bay leaf
½ lb. uncooked shrimp
  (31-40 per lb.), peeled
  and deveined and
  tails removed
½ lb. fully cooked andouille
  sausage links, sliced
⅔ cup shredded Parmesan
  cheese, optional

In a 4- or 5-qt. slow cooker, combine the first 13 ingredients. Cook, covered, on high for 1¾ hours. Stir in shrimp, sausage and, if desired, cheese. Cook until shrimp turn pink and rice is tender, 10-15 minutes longer. Remove bay leaf.

1½ CUPS: 335 cal., 11g fat (3g sat. fat), 97mg chol., 1276mg sod., 42g carb. (4g sugars, 3g fiber), 19g pro.

ROSEMARY LAMB SHANKS

When I was young my family lived in New Zealand for two years after the war. One dinner that was a big hit was this slow-cooked lamb dish. One taste always takes me back.

—*Nancy Heishman, Las Vegas, NV*

PREP: 25 MIN. • COOK: 6 HOURS • MAKES: 8 SERVINGS

1 tsp. salt
¾ tsp. pepper
4 lamb shanks (about 20 oz. each)
1 Tbsp. butter
½ cup white wine
3 medium parsnips, peeled and cut into 1-in. chunks
2 large carrots, peeled and cut into 1-in. chunks
2 medium turnips, peeled and cut into 1-in. chunks
2 large tomatoes, chopped
1 large onion, chopped
4 garlic cloves, minced
2 cups beef broth
1 pkg. (10 oz.) frozen peas, thawed
⅓ cup chopped fresh parsley
2 Tbsp. minced fresh rosemary

1. Rub salt and pepper over lamb. In a large skillet, heat butter over medium-high heat; brown meat. Transfer meat to a 6- or 7-qt. slow cooker. Add wine to skillet; cook and stir 1 minute to loosen brown bits. Pour over lamb. Add the parsnips, carrots, turnips, tomatoes, onion, garlic and broth. Cook, covered, on low until meat is tender, 6-8 hours.

2. Remove lamb, keep warm. Stir in the peas, parsley and rosemary; heat through. Serve lamb with vegetables.

½ LAMB SHANK WITH 1 CUP VEGETABLES: 350 cal., 15g fat (6g sat. fat), 103mg chol., 668mg sod., 22g carb. (8g sugars, 6g fiber), 31g pro.

DIABETIC EXCHANGES: 4 lean meat, 1 starch, 1 vegetable, ½ fat.

HEARTY HOMEMADE CHICKEN NOODLE SOUP

This satisfying homemade soup with a hint of cayenne is brimming with vegetables, chicken and noodles. The recipe came from my father-in-law, but I made some adjustments to give it my own spin.

—Norma Reynolds, Overland Park, KS

PREP: 20 MIN. • COOK: 5½ HOURS • MAKES: 12 SERVINGS (3 QT.)

12 fresh baby carrots,
    cut into ½-in. pieces
4 celery ribs, cut into
    ½-in. pieces
¾ cup finely chopped onion
1 Tbsp. minced
    fresh parsley
½ tsp. pepper
¼ tsp. cayenne pepper
1½ tsp. mustard seed
2 garlic cloves, peeled
    and halved
1¼ lbs. boneless skinless
    chicken breast halves
1¼ lbs. boneless skinless
    chicken thighs
4 cans (14½ oz. each)
    chicken broth
1 pkg. (9 oz.) refrigerated
    linguine
    Optional: Coarsely
    ground pepper and
    additional minced fresh
    parsley

1. In a 5-qt. slow cooker, combine the first 6 ingredients. Place mustard seed and garlic on a double thickness of cheesecloth; bring up corners of cloth and tie with kitchen string to form a bag. Place in slow cooker. Add chicken and broth. Cover and cook on low until meat is tender, 5-6 hours.

2. Discard spice bag. Remove chicken; cool slightly. Stir linguine into soup; cover and cook on high until tender, about 30 minutes. Cut the chicken into pieces and return to soup; heat through. Sprinkle with coarsely ground pepper and additional parsley if desired.

1 CUP: 199 cal., 6g fat (2g sat. fat), 73mg chol., 663mg sod., 14g carb. (2g sugars, 1g fiber), 22g pro.

DIABETIC EXCHANGES: 3 lean meat, 1 starch.

SLOW-COOKER PEAR BUTTER

This is a tasty spread for toast, muffins, biscuits or any of your favorite breads.
It is easy to make and has a rich pear flavor with hints of cinnamon, star anise and lemon.
—*Geraldine Saucier, Albuquerque, NM*

PREP: 25 MIN. • COOK: 6 HOURS • MAKES: 6 CUPS

1 cinnamon stick (3 in.)
4-5 star anise points
    (about ½ whole)
5 lbs. pears, peeled and
    chopped (about 12 cups)
1 cup packed light
    brown sugar
1 tsp. grated lemon zest

1. Place spices on a double thickness of cheesecloth. Gather corners of cloth to enclose spices; tie securely with string. In a 5- or 6-qt. slow cooker, toss remaining ingredients. Add spice bag, covering with pears.

2. Cook, covered, on low until pears are tender, 5-6 hours. Remove spice bag.

3. Puree pear mixture using an immersion blender. Or, cool slightly and puree mixture in a blender in batches; return to slow cooker.

4. Cook, uncovered, on high until mixture is thickened to desired consistency, 1-2 hours, stirring occasionally. Store cooled pear butter in an airtight container in the refrigerator up to 1 week.

FREEZE OPTION: Freeze cooled pear butter in freezer containers up to 3 months. Liquids expand as they freeze, so leave extra room at the top of the freezer container. To use, thaw in the refrigerator.

2 TBSP.: 41 cal., 0 fat (0 sat. fat), 0 chol., 2mg sod., 11g carb. (9g sugars, 1g fiber), 0 pro.

KITCHEN TIP: To turn this into a pear sauce, which is thinner than spreadable pear butter, cook for a shorter time after pureeing.

CLOCKWISE FROM RIGHT:

A BUSHEL AND A PECK

"Our granddaughter, Morgan, wore a pretty dress to visit her buddy Si in our friends' pasture. She loves riding the gentle giant in local horse shows."

—*Kim and Sam Warren, Blairsville, Georgia*

SUNNY DISPOSITION

"As we drove past a sunflower field, my husband couldn't believe it when I wanted to stop to ask the owners if we could photograph their flowers. But, after all, anyone who grows sunflowers must be a wonderful person. The owners welcomed us to photograph there for as long as we wanted. This shot is my favorite."

—*Denise McQuillan, Fort Wayne, Indiana*

SHOTGUN!

"We bought this Jersey calf in the winter. It was too cold to haul him in the back of the truck, so he rode in the front cab where it was nice and warm!"

—*Lorianne Ende, Rogers, Minnesota*

TWICE AS NICE
"This double rainbow appeared over our property after a short storm."
—James Doughty,
Hot Springs, Arkansas

SLOW-COOKED HAM WITH PINEAPPLE SAUCE

We serve this dish during the holidays because everyone is crazy about it.
But we also enjoy it all year long because it's super simple to prepare.

—Terry Roberts, Yorktown, VA

PREP: 10 MIN. • COOK: 6 HOURS • MAKES: 12 SERVINGS

1 fully cooked boneless
  ham (4 to 5 lbs.)
1 Tbsp. cornstarch
2 Tbsp. lemon juice
1 cup packed brown sugar
1 Tbsp. yellow mustard
¼ tsp. salt
1 can (20 oz.) unsweetened
  crushed pineapple,
  undrained

1. Place ham in a 5-qt. slow cooker. In a small saucepan, mix cornstarch and lemon juice until smooth. Stir in remaining ingredients; bring to a boil, stirring occasionally. Pour over ham, covering completely.

2. Cook, covered, on low 6-8 hours (a thermometer inserted in ham should read at least 140°).

4 OZ. HAM WITH ¼ CUP SAUCE: 262 cal., 6g fat (2g sat. fat), 77mg chol., 1638mg sod., 27g carb. (25g sugars, 0 fiber), 28g pro.

NOTE: This recipe is not recommended for a spiral-sliced ham.

SHREDDED LAMB SLIDERS

I like these sliders because they taste great and feed a crowd. I actually made about
1,500 of them for a beer fest once, and they disappeared in no time.

—Craig Kuczek, Aurora, CO

PREP: 45 MIN. • **COOK:** 6 HOURS • **MAKES:** 2 DOZEN

1 **boneless lamb shoulder
   roast (3½ to 4¼ lbs.)**
1½ **tsp. salt**
½ **tsp. pepper**
1 **Tbsp. olive oil**
2 **medium carrots, chopped**
4 **shallots, chopped**
6 **garlic cloves**
2 **cups beef stock**

PESTO
¾ **cup fresh mint leaves**
¾ **cup loosely packed
   basil leaves**
⅓ **cup pine nuts**
¼ **tsp. salt**
¾ **cup olive oil**
¾ **cup shredded
   Parmesan cheese**
⅓ **cup shredded
   Asiago cheese**
24 **slider buns**
1 **pkg. (4 oz.) crumbled
   feta cheese**

1. Sprinkle roast with salt and pepper. In a large skillet, heat oil over medium-high heat; brown meat. Transfer meat to a 6- or 7-qt. slow cooker. In the same skillet, cook and stir carrots, shallots and garlic until crisp-tender, about 4 minutes. Add stock, stirring to loosen browned bits from pan. Pour over lamb. Cook, covered, on low until lamb is tender, 6-8 hours.

2. Meanwhile for pesto, place mint, basil, pine nuts and salt in a food processor; pulse until chopped. Continue processing while gradually adding oil in a steady stream. Add Parmesan and Asiago cheeses; pulse just until blended.

3. When cool enough to handle, remove meat from bones; discard bones. Shred meat with 2 forks. Strain cooking juices, adding vegetables to shredded meat; skim fat. Return cooking juices and meat to slow cooker. Heat through. Serve on buns with pesto and feta.

1 SLIDER: 339 cal., 22g fat (7g sat. fat), 56mg chol., 459mg sod., 16g carb. (2g sugars, 1g fiber), 18g pro.

SLOW-COOKED LASAGNA SOUP

Every fall and winter, our staff has a soup rotation. I modified this recipe so I can
prep it the night before and put it in the slow cooker in the morning. My colleagues love it!
—Sharon Gerst, North Liberty, IA

PREP: 35 MIN. • COOK: 5 HOURS + STANDING • MAKES: 8 SERVINGS (2½ QT.)

1 pkg. (19½ oz.) Italian
   turkey sausage links,
   casings removed
1 large onion, chopped
2 medium carrots, chopped
2 cups sliced fresh
   mushrooms
3 garlic cloves, minced
1 carton (32 oz.) reduced-
   sodium chicken broth
2 cans (14½ oz. each)
   no-salt-added
   stewed tomatoes
2 cans (8 oz. each) no-salt-
   added tomato sauce
2 tsp. Italian seasoning
6 lasagna noodles, broken
   into 1-in. pieces
2 cups coarsely chopped
   fresh spinach
1 cup cubed or
   shredded part-skim
   mozzarella cheese
   Optional: Shredded
   Parmesan cheese and
   minced fresh basil

1. In a large skillet, cook sausage over medium-high heat,
breaking into crumbles, until no longer pink, 8-10 minutes;
drain. Transfer to a 5- or 6-qt. slow cooker.

2. Add onion and carrots to same skillet; cook and stir until
softened, 2-4 minutes. Stir in mushrooms and garlic; cook and
stir until mushrooms are softened, 2-4 minutes. Transfer to
slow cooker. Stir in broth, tomatoes, tomato sauce and Italian
seasoning. Cook, covered, on low until vegetables are tender,
4-6 hours.

3. Add noodles; cook until tender, 1 hour longer. Stir in spinach.
Remove insert; let stand 10 minutes. Divide mozzarella cheese
among serving bowls; ladle soup over cheese. If desired,
sprinkle with Parmesan cheese and basil.

1⅓ CUPS: 266 cal., 8g fat (3g sat. fat), 36mg chol., 725mg sod., 30g
carb. (11g sugars, 5g fiber), 18g pro.

DIABETIC EXCHANGES: 2 vegetable, 2 lean meat, 1½ starch.

CHERRY UPSIDE-DOWN BREAD PUDDING

I've always loved bread pudding, and I enjoy fixing this for my family on a chilly day. For a completely different dessert, use another flavor of pie filling and omit the chocolate chips.

—*Ronna Farley, Rockville, MD*

PREP: 20 MIN. + COOLING • **COOK:** 2¾ HOURS • **MAKES:** 12 SERVINGS

1 loaf (16 oz.) sliced white bread
1 can (21 oz.) cherry pie filling
½ cup butter, softened
1 cup sugar
5 large eggs, room temperature
2 cups 2% milk
1 tsp. ground cinnamon
1 tsp. vanilla extract
¾ cup semisweet chocolate chips
Sweetened whipped cream, optional

1. Place bread slices on ungreased baking sheets. Broil each pan 3-4 in. from heat until golden brown, 1-2 minutes on each side; let cool. Cut into 1-in. pieces; set aside.

2. Spoon pie filling into a greased 5- or 6-qt. slow cooker. In a large bowl cream butter and sugar until crumbly. Add 1 egg at a time, beating well after each addition. Beat in milk, cinnamon and vanilla (mixture may appear curdled). Gently stir in the chocolate chips and the bread cubes; let stand until bread is softened, about 10 minutes. Transfer to slow cooker.

3. Cook, covered, on low until set and a knife inserted in the center comes out clean, 2¾-3¼ hours. Serve warm, with whipped cream if desired.

¾ CUP: 393 cal., 15g fat (8g sat. fat), 101mg chol., 305mg sod., 58g carb. (27g sugars, 2g fiber), 8g pro.

COOKIES, BARS & BROWNIES

Warm and fresh from the oven, these treats satisfy every time.
Share them with a neighbor, take them to the bake sale or simply
load up your cookie jar and enjoy the smiles that promise to follow.

GRANDMA'S SCOTTISH SHORTBREAD

My Scottish grandmother was renowned for her baking, and one of the highlights whenever we visited were her shortbread cookies. Whenever I make them, I think of her. Try them with a cup of tea.

—*Jane Kelly, Wayland, MA*

PREP: 15 MIN. • **BAKE:** 45 MIN. + COOLING • **MAKES:** 4 DOZEN

1 lb. butter, softened

8 oz. superfine sugar (about 1¼ cups)

1 lb. all-purpose flour (3⅔ cups)

8 oz. white rice flour (1⅓ cups)

1. Preheat oven to 300°. Cream butter and sugar until light and fluffy, 5-7 minutes. Combine flours; gradually beat into creamed mixture. Press dough into an ungreased 13x9-in. baking pan. Prick with a fork.

2. Bake until light brown, 45-50 minutes. Cut into 48 bars or triangles while warm. Cool completely on a wire rack.

1 BAR: 139 cal., 8g fat (5g sat. fat), 20mg chol., 61mg sod., 16g carb. (5g sugars, 0 fiber), 1g pro.

CHOCOLATE GINGERSNAPS

When my daughter Jennifer was 15 years old, she created this recipe as a way to combine two of her favorite flavors. Grab a cold glass of milk and enjoy!

—Paula Zsiray, Logan, UT

PREP: 45 MIN. + CHILLING • BAKE: 10 MIN./BATCH • MAKES: ABOUT 3½ DOZEN

½ cup butter, softened
½ cup packed light
   brown sugar
¼ cup molasses
1 Tbsp. water
2 tsp. minced fresh
   gingerroot
1½ cups all-purpose flour
1 Tbsp. baking cocoa
1¼ tsp. ground ginger
1 tsp. baking soda
1 tsp. ground cinnamon
¼ tsp. ground nutmeg
¼ tsp. ground cloves
7 oz. semisweet chocolate,
   finely chopped
¼ cup coarse sugar

1. In a large bowl, cream butter and brown sugar until light and fluffy, 5-7 minutes. Beat in the molasses, water and gingerroot. Combine the flour, baking cocoa, ginger, baking soda, cinnamon, nutmeg and cloves; gradually add to creamed mixture and mix well. Stir in the chocolate. Cover and refrigerate until easy to handle, about 2 hours.

2. Shape dough into 1-in. balls; roll in coarse sugar. Place 2 in. apart on greased baking sheets.

3. Bake at 350° until tops begin to crack, 10-12 minutes. Cool for 2 minutes before removing to wire racks.

1 COOKIE: 80 cal., 4g fat (2g sat. fat), 6mg chol., 47mg sod., 9g carb. (6g sugars, 0 fiber), 1g pro.

BLUEBERRY LATTICE BARS

Since our area has an annual blueberry festival, my daughters and I are always looking for new berry recipes to enter in the baking contest. These lovely, yummy bars won a blue ribbon one year.

—Debbie Ayers, Baileyville, ME

PREP: 25 MIN. + CHILLING • BAKE: 30 MIN. • MAKES: 2 DOZEN

1⅓ cups butter, softened
⅔ cup sugar
¼ tsp. salt
1 large egg, room temperature
½ tsp. vanilla extract
3¾ cups all-purpose flour

FILLING
3 cups fresh or frozen blueberries
1 cup sugar
3 Tbsp. cornstarch

1. Cream butter, sugar and salt until light and fluffy, 5-7 minutes; beat in egg and vanilla. Gradually beat in flour. Divide dough in half; shape each into a 1-in.-thick rectangle. Wrap and refrigerate 2 hours or overnight.

2. Preheat oven to 375°. Place the blueberries, sugar and cornstarch in a small saucepan. Bring to a boil over medium heat, stirring frequently; cook and stir until thickened, about 2 minutes. Cool slightly.

3. Roll each portion of dough between 2 sheets of waxed paper into a 14x10-in. rectangle. Place rectangles on separate baking sheets; freeze until firm, 5-10 minutes. Place 1 rectangle in a greased 13x9-in. baking pan, pressing onto bottom and about ½ in. up the sides. Add filling.

4. Cut remaining rectangle into ½-in. strips; freeze 5-10 minutes to firm. Arrange strips over the filling in crisscross fashion. If desired, press edges with a fork to seal strips. Bake until top crust is golden brown, 30-35 minutes. Cool on a wire rack. Cut into bars.

1 BAR: 233 cal., 11g fat (7g sat. fat), 35mg chol., 109mg sod., 32g carb. (16g sugars, 1g fiber), 3g pro.

ALL IN THE FAMILY
"I was in New Mexico taking photos of wild horses when I came upon a small herd of mustangs grazing on the open range. As I got a little closer, I captured this shot of the stallion and his mares. Having the opportunity to be out in nature, moving among this herd of animals, is an experience I will never forget."
—*Jerry Cowart, Chatsworth, California*

FROM TOP:

GLORIOUS GAMBREL
"I drove to Burlington, Washington, one day. A friend had given me a tip about this beautiful Dutch gambrel barn that was built in the late 1930s, and I had to snap a pic."
—*Jeff Schenekl, Arlington, Washington*

TWO OF A PAIR
"Clyde, our rescue pup, quickly bonded with our daughter Israella. It was love at first sight, and now the two of them are seldom apart. There sure is a lot of laughter in our home!"
—*Cathy Conder, Freeport, Illinois*

HONEY CINNAMON BARS

My Aunt Ellie gave us the recipe for these sweet old-fashioned bar cookies.
Featuring cinnamon, walnuts and honey, they're a great addition to coffee breaks.
—*Diane Myers, Star, ID*

PREP: 25 MIN. • **BAKE:** 10 MIN. + COOLING • **MAKES:** 2 DOZEN

1 **cup sugar**
¾ **cup canola oil**
¼ **cup honey**
1 **large egg, room temperature**
2 **cups all-purpose flour**
1 **tsp. baking soda**
1 **tsp. ground cinnamon**
¼ **tsp. salt**
1 **cup chopped walnuts, toasted**

GLAZE
1 **cup confectioners' sugar**
2 **Tbsp. mayonnaise**
1 **tsp. vanilla extract**
1 **to 2 Tbsp. water**
  Additional toasted chopped walnuts, optional

1. Preheat oven to 350°. In a large bowl, beat sugar, oil, honey and egg until well blended. In another bowl, whisk flour, baking soda, cinnamon and salt; gradually beat into sugar mixture. Stir in 1 cup walnuts.

2. Spread into a greased 15x10x1-in. baking pan. Bake until golden brown (edges will puff up), 10-12 minutes. Cool completely on a wire rack.

3. For glaze, in a small bowl, mix confectioners' sugar, mayonnaise, vanilla and enough water to reach desired consistency; spread over the top. If desired, sprinkle with the additional walnuts. Let stand until set. Cut into bars. Refrigerate leftovers.

1 BAR: 206 cal., 11g fat (1g sat. fat), 8mg chol., 86mg sod., 25g carb. (16g sugars, 1g fiber), 2g pro.

LEMONY GINGERBREAD WHOOPIE PIES

These whoopie pies are spiced just right. They combine two popular flavors in one fun treat. I roll the chewy cookies in sugar before baking for a bit of crunch.

—Jamie Jones, Madison, GA

PREP: 25 MIN. + CHILLING • **BAKE:** 10 MIN./BATCH + COOLING • **MAKES:** ABOUT 2 DOZEN

¾ cup butter, softened
¾ cup packed brown sugar
½ cup molasses
1 large egg, room temperature
3 cups all-purpose flour
2 tsp. ground ginger
1 tsp. ground cinnamon
1 tsp. baking soda
¼ tsp. salt
½ cup sugar

FILLING
¾ cup butter, softened
¾ cup marshmallow creme
1½ cups confectioners' sugar
¾ tsp. lemon extract

1. In a large bowl, cream butter and brown sugar until light and fluffy, 5-7 minutes. Beat in molasses and egg. Combine flour, ginger, cinnamon, baking soda and salt; gradually add to the creamed mixture and mix well. Cover and refrigerate for at least 3 hours.

2. Preheat oven to 350°. Shape the dough into 1-in. balls; roll in sugar. Place 3 in. apart on ungreased baking sheets. Flatten to ½-in. thickness with a glass dipped in sugar. Bake 8-10 minutes or until set. Cool 2 minutes before removing from pans to wire racks to cool completely.

3. For filling, in a small bowl, beat butter and marshmallow creme until light and fluffy. Gradually beat in confectioners' sugar and extract.

4. Spread filling on the bottoms of half of the cookies, about 1 Tbsp. on each; top with remaining cookies.

1 WHOOPIE PIE: 286 cal., 13g fat (8g sat. fat), 42mg chol., 184mg sod., 41g carb. (26g sugars, 1g fiber), 2g pro.

FUDGY LAYERED IRISH MOCHA BROWNIES

My husband and I are big fans of Irish cream, so I wanted to incorporate it into a brownie.
I started with my mom's brownie recipe, then added frosting and ganache.

—*Sue Gronholz, Beaver Dam, WI*

PREP: 35 MIN. • BAKE: 25 MIN. + CHILLING • MAKES: 16 SERVINGS

⅔ cup all-purpose flour
½ tsp. baking powder
¼ tsp. salt
⅓ cup butter
6 Tbsp. baking cocoa
2 Tbsp. canola oil
½ tsp. instant coffee
   granules
1 cup sugar
2 large eggs, room
   temperature, beaten
1 tsp. vanilla extract

FROSTING
2 cups confectioners' sugar
¼ cup butter, softened
3 Tbsp. Irish cream liqueur

GANACHE TOPPING
1 cup semisweet
   chocolate chips
3 Tbsp. Irish cream liqueur
2 Tbsp. heavy
   whipping cream
½ tsp. instant coffee
   granules

1. Preheat oven to 350°. Sift together flour, baking powder and salt; set aside. In a small saucepan over low heat, melt butter. Remove from heat; stir in cocoa, oil and instant coffee granules. Cool slightly; stir in sugar and beaten eggs. Gradually add flour mixture and vanilla; mix well. Spread batter into a greased 8-in. square pan; bake until the center is set (do not overbake), about 25 minutes. Cool in pan on wire rack.

2. For frosting, whisk together the confectioners' sugar and butter (mixture will be lumpy). Gradually whisk in Irish cream liqueur; beat until smooth. Spread over slightly warm brownies. Refrigerate until frosting is set, about 1 hour.

3. Meanwhile, prepare the ganache: Combine all ingredients and microwave on high for 1 minute; stir. Microwave 30 seconds longer; stir until smooth. Cool slightly until ganache reaches a spreading consistency. Spread over the frosting. Refrigerate until set, 45-60 minutes.

1 BROWNIE: 295 cal., 14g fat (7g sat. fat), 43mg chol., 116mg sod., 41g carb. (34g sugars, 1g fiber), 2g pro.

GRANDMA BRUBAKER'S ORANGE COOKIES

At least two generations of my family have enjoyed the recipe for these light, delicate, orange-flavored cookies. The icing makes them special, but they're also delightful plain.
—*Sheri DeBolt, Huntington, IN*

PREP: 20 MIN. • BAKE: 10 MIN./BATCH + COOLING • MAKES: ABOUT 6 DOZEN

1 cup shortening
2 cups sugar
2 large eggs, separated, room temperature
1 cup buttermilk
5 cups all-purpose flour
2 tsp. baking powder
2 tsp. baking soda
   Pinch salt
   Juice and grated zest of 2 medium navel oranges

ICING
2 cups confectioners' sugar
¼ cup orange juice
1 Tbsp. butter
1 Tbsp. grated orange zest

1. Preheat oven to 325°. In a bowl, cream shortening and sugar. Beat in egg yolks and buttermilk. Sift together flour, baking powder, soda and salt; add to creamed mixture alternately with orange juice and zest. Add egg whites and beat until smooth.

2. Drop by rounded teaspoonfuls onto greased cookie sheets. Bake until set, about 10 minutes. Remove to wire racks to cool completely.

3. For icing, combine all ingredients and beat until smooth. Frost cooled cookies.

1 COOKIE: 97 cal., 3g fat (1g sat. fat), 6mg chol., 58mg sod., 16g carb. (9g sugars, 0 fiber), 1g pro.

BLUE RIBBON WINNER

PEPPERMINT BROWNIES

My grandmother encouraged me to enter these mint brownies in the county fair some years ago, and they earned top honors! They're a delicious treat to serve during the holidays.

—Marcy Greenblatt, Redding, CA

PREP: 15 MIN. • **BAKE:** 35 MIN. + COOLING. • **MAKES:** 2 DOZEN

1⅓ cups all-purpose flour
1 cup baking cocoa
1 tsp. salt
1 tsp. baking powder
¾ cup canola oil
2 cups sugar
2 tsp. vanilla extract
4 large eggs, room temperature
⅔ cup crushed peppermint candies

GLAZE
1 cup semisweet chocolate chips
1 Tbsp. shortening
2 Tbsp. crushed peppermint candies

1. Preheat oven to 350°. Line a 13x9-in. baking pan with foil; grease lining.

2. In a bowl, whisk together first 4 ingredients. In a large bowl, beat oil and sugar until blended. Beat in vanilla and 1 egg at a time, beating well after each addition. Gradually add the flour mixture; stir in peppermint candies. Spread into prepared pan.

3. Bake until a toothpick inserted in center comes out clean, 35-40 minutes. Cool in pan on a wire rack.

4. In a microwave, melt chocolate chips and shortening; stir until smooth. Spread over brownies; sprinkle with candies.

1 BROWNIE: 222 cal., 11g fat (3g sat. fat), 35mg chol., 128mg sod., 31g carb. (22g sugars, 1g fiber), 3g pro.

LIVING THE 'CRANBERRY WAY'

STORY BY SANDY POTTER NEMITZ AND DAVID POTTER WARRENS, WISCONSIN

We are a brother-and-sister team continuing the family legacy of growing cranberries. I'm Sandy, and my brother David and I grew up on the family marsh, learning and living the "cranberry way." Now we are seventh-generation cranberry growers in Wisconsin, the country's top cranberry-producing state. I'm proud to say that we Potters are the longest continuous line of cranberry growers in the state.

Our family's marsh, the James Potter Cranberry Marsh, is in Warrens. David and his family live next door. My husband, Adam Nemitz, and I live on a marsh that Adam's family owns.

My brother and I work full time for our dad, Todd Potter. Our dad and grandmother spend a lot of time teaching us as many farming skills as they can. We often laugh because any time Dad steps in to help, he makes it look so easy.

David manages the marshes, and I manage the business end of things. We are both down in the cranberry beds daily, however, getting our hands dirty and learning new skills.

As the seasons change, so do our job descriptions. Winter months are spent maintaining equipment and renovating and sanding the beds. Spring is all about irrigation, frost watches, and gearing up for cranberry blossoms and bees. Summer is packed with irrigating, fertilizing, spraying and mowing. Fall means harvest. There is nothing we anticipate more than getting our 210 acres of cranberries harvested. We take a great deal of pride in our work and in watching our marsh and family grow from year to year. Our parents and grandparents put their hearts into the family business, and we hope to see the James Potter Cranberry Marsh handed down to our own children someday.

Opposite and top: Sandy Nemitz moves ramps with a tractor so a harrow can drive into flooded cranberry beds. Bottom left: Todd Potter (center) with Sandy Nemitz and David Potter. Bottom right: The berry pump (center) sucks up the floating cranberries and sorts them from stray leaves and vines. Berries then go in the semitruck (left) and debris moves to the "trash truck" (right).

CRANBERRY BOG BARS

Sweet and chewy, these fun bars combine the flavors of oats, cranberries, brown sugar and pecans. I like to sprinkle the squares with confectioners' sugar before serving.

—Sally Wakefield, Gans, PA

PREP: 25 MIN. • BAKE: 25 MIN. • MAKES: 2 DOZEN

1¼ cups butter, softened, divided
1½ cups packed brown sugar, divided
3½ cups old-fashioned oats, divided
1 cup all-purpose flour
1 can (14 oz.) whole-berry cranberry sauce
½ cup finely chopped pecans

1. In a large bowl, cream 1 cup butter and 1 cup brown sugar until light and fluffy, 5-7 minutes. Combine 2½ cups oats and flour. Gradually add to the creamed mixture until crumbly. Press into a greased 13x9-in. baking pan. Spread with the cranberry sauce.

2. In a microwave-safe bowl, melt remaining butter; stir in the pecans and remaining brown sugar and oats. Sprinkle over cranberry sauce. Bake at 375° 25-30 minutes or until lightly browned. Cool on a wire rack. Cut into bars.

1 BAR: 239 cal., 12g fat (6g sat. fat), 25mg chol., 88mg sod., 32g carb. (18g sugars, 2g fiber), 2g pro.

CHEWY GOOD OATMEAL COOKIES

Here's a classic oatmeal cookie with all of my favorite extras: dried cherries,
white chocolate chips and chopped macadamia nuts.

—Sandy Harz, Spring Lake, MI

PREP: 20 MIN. • BAKE: 10 MIN./BATCH • MAKES: 3½ DOZEN

1 cup butter, softened
1 cup packed brown sugar
½ cup sugar
2 large eggs, room
   temperature
1 Tbsp. honey
2 tsp. vanilla extract
2½ cups quick-cooking oats
1½ cups all-purpose flour
1 tsp. baking soda
½ tsp. salt
½ tsp. ground cinnamon
1⅓ cups dried cherries
1 cup white baking chips
1 cup (4 oz.) chopped
   macadamia nuts

BLUE RIBBON WINNER

1. Preheat oven to 350°. In a large bowl, cream the butter and sugars until light and fluffy, 5-7 minutes. Beat in eggs, honey and vanilla. In another bowl, mix the oats, flour, baking soda, salt and cinnamon; gradually beat into creamed mixture. Stir in the remaining ingredients.

2. Drop dough by rounded tablespoonfuls 2 in. apart onto greased baking sheets. Bake 10-12 minutes or until golden brown. Cool on pan 2 minutes; remove to wire racks to cool.

1 COOKIE: 161 cal., 8g fat (4g sat. fat), 22mg chol., 105mg sod., 20g carb. (13g sugars, 1g fiber), 2g pro.

CHEWY GOOD CRANBERRY OATMEAL COOKIES: Substitute dried cranberries for the dried cherries.

CHEWY GOOD OATMEAL CHIP COOKIES: Omit the cinnamon, dried cherries and macadamia nuts. Add 1 cup each semisweet chocolate chips and butterscotch chips along with the white baking chips.

MINI S'MORES

Want to sink your teeth into s'mores all year long? Here's the answer! Just combine marshmallow creme, chocolate, graham crackers and a few other items for an awesome treat.

—Stephanie Tewell, Elizabeth, IL

PREP: 50 MIN. + STANDING • COOK: 5 MIN. • MAKES: ABOUT 4 DOZEN

2 cups milk chocolate chips
½ cup heavy whipping cream
1 pkg. (14.4 oz.) graham crackers, quartered
1 cup marshmallow creme
2 cartons (7 oz. each) milk chocolate for dipping
4 oz. white candy coating, melted, optional

1. Place chocolate chips in a small bowl. In a small saucepan, bring cream just to a boil. Pour over chocolate; stir with a whisk until smooth. Cool to room temperature or until mixture reaches a spreading consistency, about 10 minutes.

2. Spread chocolate mixture over half of the graham crackers. Spread marshmallow creme over remaining graham crackers; place over chocolate-covered crackers, pressing to adhere.

3. Melt dipping chocolate according to package directions. Dip each s'more halfway into dipping chocolate; allow excess to drip off. Place on waxed paper-lined baking sheets; let stand until dipping chocolate is set.

4. If desired, drizzle tops with melted white candy coating; let stand until set. Store in an airtight container in the refrigerator.

1 PIECE: 145 cal., 7g fat (4g sat. fat), 5mg chol., 66mg sod., 19g carb. (13g sugars, 1g fiber), 2g pro.

KITCHEN TIP: Keep on whisking! At first, the chocolate and cream mixture may look separated. But don't panic—it will smooth out with plenty of whisking.

CHERRY CHOCOLATE CHUNK COOKIES

These rich, fudgy cookies are chewy and studded with tangy dried cherries. It's a good thing the recipe makes only a small batch, because we eat them all in one night!

—*Trisha Kruse, Eagle, ID*

PREP: 15 MIN. • BAKE: 15 MIN./BATCH • MAKES: ABOUT 1½ DOZEN

½ cup butter, softened
¾ cup sugar
1 large egg, room temperature
2 Tbsp. 2% milk
½ tsp. vanilla extract
1 cup all-purpose flour
6 Tbsp. baking cocoa
¼ tsp. baking soda
¼ tsp. salt
1 cup semisweet chocolate chunks
½ cup dried cherries

1. Preheat oven to 350°. Cream butter and sugar until light and fluffy, 5-7 minutes. Beat in egg, milk and vanilla. In a separate bowl, whisk flour, cocoa, baking soda and salt; gradually beat into creamed mixture. Stir in chocolate and cherries.

2. Drop by rounded tablespoonfuls 2 in. apart onto baking sheets lightly coated with cooking spray. Bake 12-14 minutes or until firm. Cool for 1 minute before removing to a wire rack.

1 COOKIE: 159 cal., 8g fat (5g sat. fat), 22mg chol., 88mg sod., 22g carb. (15g sugars, 1g fiber), 2g pro.

STRAWBERRY RHUBARB CHEESECAKE BARS

These cheesecake bars layer a buttery pecan shortbread crust with a rich and creamy filling and sweet-tart strawberry rhubarb jam. For larger squares, cut into nine bars.

—Amanda Scarlati, Sandy, UT

PREP: 30 MIN. + CHILLING • **BAKE:** 15 MIN. + COOLING • **MAKES:** 16 SERVINGS

1 cup all-purpose flour
⅓ cup packed brown sugar
Dash kosher salt
½ cup cold butter, cubed
⅓ cup finely chopped pecans

FILLING
1 pkg. (8 oz.) cream cheese, softened
¼ cup sugar
2 Tbsp. 2% milk
1 Tbsp. lemon juice
½ tsp. vanilla extract
Dash kosher salt
1 large egg, room temperature, lightly beaten

JAM
½ cup sugar
2 Tbsp. cornstarch
1⅓ cups chopped fresh strawberries
1⅓ cups sliced fresh or frozen rhubarb
1 Tbsp. lemon juice

1. Preheat oven to 350°. Line an 8-in. square baking pan with parchment, letting ends extend up sides. In a small bowl, mix flour, brown sugar and salt; cut in butter until crumbly. Stir in the pecans.

2. Press into bottom of prepared pan. Bake until edges just begin to brown, 12-15 minutes. Cool completely on a wire rack.

3. In a large bowl, beat cream cheese and sugar until smooth. Beat in milk, lemon juice, vanilla and salt. Add egg; beat on low speed just until blended. Pour over crust.

4. Bake until filling is set, 15-20 minutes. Cool on a wire rack for 1 hour.

5. For jam, in a small saucepan, mix sugar and cornstarch. Add strawberries, rhubarb and lemon juice. Bring to a boil. Reduce heat; simmer, uncovered, until the mixture begins to thicken, 6-8 minutes. Cool completely. Spread over filling. Refrigerate until set, 8 hours or overnight.

6. Using parchment, carefully remove cheesecake from baking pan. Cut into bars.

1 BAR: 215 cal., 13g fat (7g sat. fat), 41mg chol., 113mg sod., 24g carb. (15g sugars, 1g fiber), 3g pro.

BLUE
RIBBON
WINNER

LEMON POPPY SEED CUTOUTS

I love to package up these cookies to share with friends! You could spread buttercream or cream cheese frosting on them to make sandwich cookies. They'd also be delicious dipped in white chocolate.

—*Ilana Pulda, Bellevue, WA*

PREP: 30 MIN. + CHILLING • **BAKE:** 10 MIN./BATCH • **MAKES:** ABOUT 3 DOZEN

1 cup unsalted
   butter, softened
½ cup confectioners' sugar
1 Tbsp. sugar
1 Tbsp. grated lemon zest
4 tsp. lemon juice
½ tsp. vanilla extract
2 cups all-purpose flour
1 Tbsp. poppy seeds
¼ tsp. salt

1. Cream butter and sugars until light and fluffy, 5-7 minutes. Beat in lemon zest, juice and vanilla. In another bowl, whisk the flour, poppy seeds and salt; gradually beat into creamed mixture. Shape into a disk; cover tightly. Refrigerate 4 hours or until firm enough to roll.

2. Preheat oven to 350°. Roll dough between 2 sheets of waxed paper to ¼-in. thickness. Cut with a floured 1½-in. cookie cutter; reroll scraps. Place 1 in. apart on parchment-lined baking sheets. Bake until edges begin to brown, 10-12 minutes. Remove from pans to wire racks to cool.

1 COOKIE: 80 cal., 5g fat (3g sat. fat), 14mg chol., 17mg sod., 7g carb. (2g sugars, 0 fiber), 1g pro.

CHAPTER 9
FAVORITE DESSERTS

There's always room for dessert when country classics round out menus. Bubbling fruit cobblers, old-fashioned pies and decadent cakes...turn the page for these sweet specialties and many more!

DOWN EAST BLUEBERRY BUCKLE

This buckle won a contest at my daughter's college. The real prize was seeing the smile on her face, and the fact that we can enjoy this heavenly treat regularly.

—Dianne van der Veen, Plymouth, MA

PREP: 15 MIN. • BAKE: 30 MIN. • MAKES: 9 SERVINGS

2 cups all-purpose flour
¾ cup sugar
2½ tsp. baking powder
¼ tsp. salt
1 large egg, room temperature
¾ cup 2% milk
¼ cup butter, melted
2 cups fresh or frozen blueberries

TOPPING
½ cup sugar
⅓ cup all-purpose flour
½ tsp. ground cinnamon
¼ cup butter, softened

1. Preheat oven to 375°. In a large bowl, whisk flour, sugar, baking powder and salt. In another bowl, whisk egg, milk and melted butter until blended. Add to flour mixture; stir just until moistened. Fold in blueberries. Transfer to a greased 9-in. square baking pan.

2. For topping, in a small bowl, mix sugar, flour and cinnamon. Using a fork, stir in softened butter until mixture is crumbly. Sprinkle over batter.

3. Bake 30-35 minutes or until a toothpick inserted in center comes out clean (do not overbake). Cool in pan on a wire rack. Serve warm or at room temperature.

1 PIECE: 354 cal., 12g fat (7g sat. fat), 49mg chol., 277mg sod., 59g carb. (32g sugars, 2g fiber), 5g pro.

BLUE
RIBBON
WINNER

HUMMINGBIRD CAKE

This impressive cake is my dad's favorite, so I always make it for his birthday. The beautiful old-fashioned layered delight makes a memorable dessert any time of year.

—Nancy Zimmerman, Cape May Court House, NJ

PREP: 40 MIN. • BAKE: 25 MIN. + COOLING • MAKES: 14 SERVINGS

2 cups mashed ripe bananas
1½ cups canola oil
3 large eggs, room temperature
1 can (8 oz.) unsweetened crushed pineapple, undrained
1½ tsp. vanilla extract
3 cups all-purpose flour
2 cups sugar
1 tsp. salt
1 tsp. baking soda
1 tsp. ground cinnamon
1 cup chopped walnuts

PINEAPPLE FROSTING

¼ cup shortening
2 Tbsp. butter, softened
1 tsp. grated lemon zest
¼ tsp. salt
6 cups confectioners' sugar
½ cup unsweetened pineapple juice
2 tsp. half-and-half cream
Chopped walnuts, optional

1. In a large bowl, beat the bananas, oil, eggs, pineapple and vanilla until well blended. In another bowl, combine the flour, sugar, salt, baking soda and cinnamon; gradually beat into banana mixture until blended. Stir in walnuts.

2. Pour into 3 greased and floured 9-in. round baking pans. Bake at 350° until a toothpick inserted in the center comes out clean, 25-30 minutes. Cool for 10 minutes before removing from pans to wire racks to cool completely.

3. For frosting, in a large bowl, beat shortening, butter, lemon zest and salt until fluffy. Add confectioners' sugar alternately with pineapple juice. Beat in cream. Spread between layers and over top and sides of cake. If desired, sprinkle with walnuts.

1 SLICE: 777 cal., 35g fat (6g sat. fat), 50mg chol., 333mg sod., 113g carb. (85g sugars, 2g fiber), 7g pro.

CLOCKWISE FROM RIGHT:

HI, MOM!
"Mama Rose was lying at the door of her hut, protecting her babies, when this little one approached with a nuzzle to let her know he was hungry."

—*Jenny Garcia, Elfrida, Arizona*

INSTANT FRIENDS
"My daughter Emily, then 3 years old, had a good laugh when our friend's baby goat named Fawn gently nibbled on her neck during a visit."

—*Hillary Sphuler, Kalispell, Montana*

TULIP TIME
"Every April, thousands of visitors arrive in Mount Vernon, Washington, from all over the world to see tulips. The Skagit Valley Tulip Festival showcases field upon field of these beautiful flowers, planted by two local growers, RoozenGaarde and Tulip Town. Both also set up spectacular display gardens for folks to enjoy. This photo was taken at Tulip Town, with one of its barns in the background."

—*Jeff Schenekl, Arlington, Washington*

BEST BUDS
"We've bottle-fed our favorite Jersey steer since he was a few days old, and he and our youngest farmer truly love each other."
—Kasey Hendrick,
Bowling Green, Kentucky

ELEGANT FRESH-BERRY TART

This tart was my first original creation. It's impressive but easy.
If other fresh fruits are used, you can adjust the simple syrup flavor to match.
—*Denise Nakamoto, Elk Grove, CA*

PREP: 45 MIN. + CHILLING • BAKE: 10 MIN. + COOLING • MAKES: 10 SERVINGS

½ cup butter, softened
⅓ cup sugar
½ tsp. grated orange zest
¼ tsp. orange extract
⅛ tsp. vanilla extract
1 cup all-purpose flour

FILLING
1 pkg. (8 oz.) cream cheese, softened
¼ cup sugar
½ tsp. lemon juice

SYRUP
2 Tbsp. water
1½ tsp. sugar
1½ tsp. red raspberry or strawberry preserves
⅛ tsp. lemon juice

TOPPING
¾ cup fresh strawberries, sliced
½ cup fresh raspberries
½ cup fresh blueberries
2 medium kiwifruit, peeled and sliced

1. Preheat oven to 375°. Cream butter and sugar until light and fluffy, 5-7 minutes. Add orange zest and extracts; gradually add flour until mixture forms a ball. Press into a greased 9-in. fluted tart pan with a removable bottom. Bake until golden brown, 10-12 minutes. Cool on a wire rack.

2. For filling, beat cream cheese, sugar and lemon juice until smooth; spread over crust. Cover and refrigerate until set, about 30 minutes.

3. Meanwhile, for the syrup, bring water, sugar, preserves and lemon juice to a boil in a small saucepan. Reduce heat; simmer, uncovered, for 10 minutes. Set aside to cool.

4. Combine strawberries, raspberries, blueberries and kiwi; toss with syrup to glaze. Arrange fruit as desired over filling. Cover and refrigerate at least 1 hour before serving.

1 SLICE: 277 cal., 17g fat (10g sat. fat), 47mg chol., 145mg sod., 29g carb. (17g sugars, 2g fiber), 3g pro.

BREAD PUDDING WITH NUTMEG

I like to make this bread pudding recipe for my dad. He says it tastes
exactly like the bread pudding with nutmeg that he so enjoyed as a child.

—Donna Powell, Montgomery City, MO

PREP: 15 MIN. • **BAKE:** 40 MIN. • **MAKES:** 6 SERVINGS

2 large eggs, room
  temperature
2 cups whole milk
¼ cup butter, cubed
¾ cup sugar
¼ tsp. salt
1 tsp. ground cinnamon
½ tsp. ground nutmeg
1 tsp. vanilla extract
4½ to 5 cups soft bread
  cubes (about 9 slices)
½ cup raisins, optional

VANILLA SAUCE
⅓ cup sugar
2 Tbsp. cornstarch
¼ tsp. salt
1⅔ cups cold water
3 Tbsp. butter
2 tsp. vanilla extract
¼ tsp. ground nutmeg

1. In a large bowl, lightly beat eggs. Combine milk and butter; add to eggs along with sugar, salt, spices and vanilla. Add bread cubes and, if desired, raisins; stir gently.

2. Pour into a well-greased 11x7-in. baking dish. Bake at 350° for 40-45 minutes or until a knife inserted 1 in. from the edge comes out clean.

3. Meanwhile, for sauce, combine the sugar, cornstarch and salt in a saucepan. Stir in water until smooth. Bring to a boil over medium heat; cook and stir until thickened, about 2 minutes. Remove from the heat. Stir in the butter, vanilla and nutmeg. Serve with warm pudding.

1 SERVING: 419 cal., 19g fat (11g sat. fat), 118mg chol., 534mg sod., 56g carb. (40g sugars, 1g fiber), 7g pro.

PEACH & BERRY COBBLER

This is one of my favorite summer recipes because it features peaches and berries that are in season, but it is just as delicious with frozen fruit. The quick biscuit topping brings it all together.

—Lauren Knoelke, Des Moines, IA

PREP: 20 MIN. • **BAKE:** 40 MIN. • **MAKES:** 8 SERVINGS

½ cup sugar
3 Tbsp. cornstarch
½ tsp. ground cinnamon
¼ tsp. ground cardamom
10 medium peaches, peeled and sliced (about 6 cups)
2 cups mixed blackberries, raspberries and blueberries
1 Tbsp. lemon juice

TOPPING
1 cup all-purpose flour
¼ cup sugar
2 tsp. grated orange zest
¾ tsp. baking powder
¼ tsp. salt
¼ tsp. baking soda
3 Tbsp. cold butter
¾ cup buttermilk
   Vanilla ice cream, optional

1. Preheat oven to 375°. In a large bowl, mix sugar, cornstarch, cinnamon and cardamom. Add peaches, berries and lemon juice; toss to combine. Transfer to a 10-in. cast-iron or other ovenproof skillet.

2. In a small bowl, whisk the first 6 topping ingredients; cut in butter until mixture resembles coarse crumbs. Add buttermilk; stir just until moistened. Drop mixture by tablespoonfuls over peach mixture.

3. Bake, uncovered, 40-45 minutes or until topping is golden brown. Serve warm. If desired, top with vanilla ice cream.

1 SERVING: 279 cal., 5g fat (3g sat. fat), 12mg chol., 238mg sod., 57g carb. (38g sugars, 5g fiber), 4g pro.

THOMAS JEFFERSON'S VANILLA ICE CREAM

The third U.S. president is credited with jotting down the first American recipe for this treat. No vanilla bean? Instead, stir 1 tablespoon vanilla extract into the cream mixture after the ice-water bath.

—Taste of Home *Test Kitchen*

PREP: 15 MIN. + CHILLING • PROCESS: 20 MIN./BATCH + FREEZING • MAKES: 2¼ QT.

2 qt. heavy whipping cream
1 cup sugar
1 vanilla bean
6 large egg yolks

1. In a large heavy saucepan, combine cream and sugar. Split vanilla bean in half lengthwise. With a sharp knife, scrape seeds into pan; add bean. Heat cream mixture over medium heat until bubbles form around sides of pan, stirring to dissolve sugar.

2. In a small bowl, whisk a small amount of the hot mixture into the egg yolks; return all to the pan, whisking constantly.

3. Cook over low heat until mixture is just thick enough to coat a metal spoon and temperature reaches 160°, stirring constantly. Do not allow to boil. Immediately transfer to a bowl.

4. Place bowl in a pan of ice water. Stir gently and occasionally for 2 minutes; discard vanilla bean. Press waxed paper onto surface of custard. Refrigerate several hours or overnight.

5. Fill cylinder of ice cream freezer two-thirds full; freeze according to the manufacturer's directions. (Refrigerate remaining mixture until ready to freeze.) Transfer ice cream to a freezer container; freeze for 4-6 hours or until firm. Repeat with remaining mixture.

½ CUP: 424 cal., 40g fat (25g sat. fat), 182mg chol., 32mg sod., 14g carb. (14g sugars, 0 fiber), 4g pro.

FAVORITE COCONUT CAKE

When I need an impressive dessert for a special occasion, this is the recipe
I depend on. My guests are glad I do! It's a coconut-lover's dream come true.
—*Edna Hoffman, Hebron, IN*

PREP: 45 MIN. • BAKE: 15 MIN. + COOLING • MAKES: 16 SERVINGS

4 large egg whites
¾ cup butter, softened
1½ cups sugar, divided
1 tsp. almond extract
1 tsp. vanilla extract
2¾ cups cake flour
4 tsp. baking powder
¾ tsp. salt
1 cup whole milk

FROSTING
5 large egg whites
1⅔ cups sugar
1 Tbsp. water
½ tsp. cream of tartar
1 tsp. vanilla extract
2½ cups unsweetened
   coconut flakes
   Colored sprinkles,
   optional

1. Place the egg whites in a large bowl; let stand at room temperature 30 minutes. Line bottoms of 3 greased 9-in. round baking pans with parchment; grease paper. Preheat oven to 350°.

2. Cream the softened butter and 1 cup sugar until light and fluffy, 5-7 minutes; beat in extracts. In another bowl, whisk together flour, baking powder and salt; add to creamed mixture alternately with milk.

3. With clean beaters, beat egg whites on medium speed until soft peaks form. Gradually add remaining sugar, 1 Tbsp. at a time, beating on high after each addition until the sugar is dissolved. Continue beating until stiff glossy peaks form. Fold into batter.

4. Transfer to prepared pans. Bake until a toothpick inserted in center comes out clean, 13-17 minutes. Cool in pans 10 minutes before removing to wire racks; remove paper. Cool completely.

5. For frosting, in a large heatproof bowl, whisk egg whites, sugar, water and cream of tartar until blended. Place over simmering water in a large saucepan over medium heat; whisking constantly, heat mixture until a thermometer reads 160°, 2-3 minutes. Remove from heat; add vanilla. Beat on high speed until stiff glossy peaks form, about 7 minutes.

6. Spread between layers and over top and sides of cake. Cover with coconut. If desired, decorate with colored sprinkles. Store, uncovered, in refrigerator.

1 SLICE: 400 cal., 16g fat (11g sat. fat), 24mg chol., 341mg sod., 62g carb. (41g sugars, 2g fiber), 5g pro.

PEANUT BUTTER ICEBOX DESSERT

Leftover crushed cookies create the yummy crust for this crowd-pleasing dessert. It's covered with a smooth cream cheese mixture, chocolate pudding and whipped topping for a lovely layered look.

—*Nancy Mueller, Highlands Ranch, CO*

PREP: 20 MIN. + CHILLING • MAKES: 15 SERVINGS

16 **Nutter Butter cookies, crushed, divided**
¼ **cup sugar**
¼ **cup butter, melted**
1 **pkg. (8 oz.) cream cheese, softened**
1⅓ **cups confectioners' sugar**
1 **carton (8 oz.) frozen whipped topping, thawed, divided**
2½ **cups cold 2% milk**
2 **pkg. (3.9 oz. each) instant chocolate pudding mix**

1. In a large bowl, combine 1¾ cups crushed cookies, sugar and butter; press into an ungreased 13x9-in. baking dish. Bake at 350° until golden brown, 6-8 minutes; cool on a wire rack.

2. In a large bowl, beat cream cheese and confectioners' sugar until smooth; fold in 1½ cups whipped topping. Spread over the cooled crust.

3. In another large bowl, beat the milk and pudding mix on low speed until thickened, about 2 minutes. Spread over the cream cheese layer. Top with remaining whipped topping; sprinkle with remaining ¼ cup crushed cookies. Cover and refrigerate for at least 1 hour before serving.

1 PIECE: 323 cal., 15g fat (9g sat. fat), 27mg chol., 217mg sod., 43g carb. (31g sugars, 1g fiber), 4g pro.

PIE...TOM SAWYER-STYLE

BY BETH HOWARD DONNELLSON, IOWA

I approach pie making in the way Tom Sawyer paints fences. Pie making is work, especially when you need to make 20 of them, as I do for our farm's annual Labor Day pig roast. Getting other people to pitch in and help is the perfect solution.

The morning of the party I round up a dozen party guests and give them a free pie lesson. Voila! A smorgasbord of homemade pies materializes for the evening's festivities.

It started by accident, 3 years ago, at a family dinner on the eve of the pig roast. A visiting relative asked if I would teach her to make pie. I had consumed one too many glasses of wine and replied, "Sure, come over at 10 a.m., and bring whomever you want." The group grew to 12 people overnight!

The group chatted and laughed that morning as we peeled apples and peaches, piling slices into pie shells. Later that day, the pie makers were the stars of the party, as guests crowded around the pie table, oohing and aahing and devouring every last crumb.

Pie is a win-win like that—it makes the baker and the eater equally happy. Which is why everyone insisted on repeating the pie marathon the next year. And the year after that.

Today, we've branched out into blueberry and strawberry pies. With so many bakers the kitchen is chaos, but there is an atmosphere of purpose and pride—and a lot of swooning over aromas from the oven. More pie means more happiness. Tom Sawyer himself would even want to help.

Left: A dozen people pack Beth Howard's farm kitchen on pie day to help with Beth's annual Labor Day Pig Roast. Above: Beth (left) calls on friends like Carolyn Agner (right) to help bake pies such as Strawberry Crumble Pie (recipe on page 317).

Pie is an art form crafted on an assembly line in Beth Howard's kitchen. Teams of friends and family make the dough before others fill and finish at least 20 pies in one morning. Above left: Strawberry Crumble Pie is one of Beth's specialties. Above right: Beth (left) and Hope Krebill (right) work on filling an apple pie, which later gets topped with a lattice crust.

STRAWBERRY CRUMBLE PIE

Pies take center stage at the end of the pig roast we host on our farm each year.
We make lots of old and new varieties, but nothing says summer like strawberries.

—Beth Howard, Donnellson, IA

PREP: 15 MIN. + CHILLING **BAKE:** 50 MIN. **MAKES:** 8 SERVINGS

1¼ cups all-purpose flour
Dash salt
¼ cup shortening
¼ cup cold butter, cube
3 to 4 Tbsp. ice water

FILLING
1 cup sugar
¼ cup quick-cooking
tapioca
Dash salt
6 cups halved fresh
strawberries

CRUMBLE
1 cup all-purpose flour
½ cup packed brown sugar
½ cup cold butter, cubed

1. In a large bowl, mix flour and salt; cut in shortening and butter until crumbly. Gradually add ice water, tossing with a fork until dough holds together when pressed. Shape into a disk; wrap. Refrigerate 1 hour or overnight.

2. Preheat oven to 425°. In a large bowl, mix sugar, tapioca and salt; add the strawberries and toss to coat. On a lightly floured surface, roll the dough to an ⅛-in.-thick circle; transfer to a 9-in. pie plate. Trim crust to ½ in. beyond rim of plate; flute edge. Add the filling.

3. For the topping, in a small bowl, combine the flour and brown sugar; cut in butter until crumbly. Sprinkle over the filling. Place on a rimmed baking sheet.

4. Bake 20-25 minutes. Reduce oven to 375°. Bake until crust is golden brown and filling is bubbly, 25-30 minutes. Cool on a wire rack.

1 SLICE: 542 cal., 24g fat (13g sat. fat), 46mg chol., 509mg sod., 79g carb. (44g sugars, 3g fiber), 5g pro.

FAVORITE PUMPKIN CAKE ROLL

Keep this cake roll in the freezer for a quick dessert for family, in case unexpected guests drop by, when you need a quick bake-sale contribution or if you're looking for a yummy hostess gift.

—Erica Berchtold, Freeport, IL

PREP: 30 MIN. • BAKE: 15 MIN. + FREEZING • MAKES: 10 SERVINGS

3 large eggs, separated, room temperature
1 cup sugar, divided
⅔ cup canned pumpkin
¾ cup all-purpose flour
1 tsp. baking soda
½ tsp. ground cinnamon
⅛ tsp. salt

FILLING
8 oz. cream cheese, softened
2 Tbsp. butter, softened
1 cup confectioners' sugar
¾ tsp. vanilla extract
Additional confectioners' sugar, optional

1. Line a 15x10x1-in. baking pan with waxed paper; grease the paper and set aside. In a large bowl, beat the egg yolks on high speed until thick and lemon-colored. Gradually add ½ cup sugar and pumpkin, beating on high until sugar is almost dissolved.

2. In a small bowl, beat the egg whites until soft peaks form. Gradually add remaining sugar, beating until stiff peaks form. Fold into egg yolk mixture. Combine the flour, baking soda, cinnamon and salt; gently fold into pumpkin mixture. Spread into prepared pan.

3. Bake at 375° until cake springs back when lightly touched, 12-15 minutes. Cool for 5 minutes. Turn cake onto a kitchen towel dusted with confectioners' sugar. Gently peel off waxed paper. Roll up cake in the towel jelly-roll style, starting with a short side. Cool completely on a wire rack.

4. In a small bowl, beat the cream cheese, butter, confectioners' sugar and vanilla until smooth. Unroll cake; spread filling evenly to within ½ in. of edges. Roll up again, without towel. Cover and freeze until firm. May be frozen for up to 3 months. Remove from the freezer 15 minutes before cutting. If desired, dust with confectioners' sugar.

1 SLICE: 285 cal., 12g fat (7g sat. fat), 94mg chol., 261mg sod., 41g carb. (32g sugars, 1g fiber), 5g pro.

KITCHEN TIP: Add extra flavor to the already-delicious filling. Swirl in apricot preserves, blackberry jam or even apple butter.

GLAZED CHOCOLATE ANGEL FOOD CAKE

Light as air and loaded with big chocolate flavor, this low-fat dessert will become a standby at all your gatherings. Add fresh strawberries or raspberries and a dollop of sweetened whipped cream if desired.

—*Mary Relyea, Canastota, NY*

PREP: 20 MIN. • BAKE: 40 MIN. + COOLING • MAKES: 12 SERVINGS

1½ cups egg whites
    (about 10 large)
1   cup cake flour
2   cups sugar, divided
½   cup baking cocoa
1   tsp. cream of tartar
1   tsp. vanilla extract
¼   tsp. salt

GLAZE
½   cup semisweet
    chocolate chips
3   Tbsp. half-and-
    half cream

1. Place egg whites in a large bowl; let stand at room temperature 30 minutes.

2. Preheat oven to 350°. Sift flour, 1 cup sugar and cocoa together twice.

3. Add cream of tartar, vanilla and salt to egg whites; beat on medium speed until soft peaks form. Gradually add remaining sugar, 2 Tbsp. at a time, beating on high after each addition until sugar is dissolved. Continue beating until stiff glossy peaks form. Gradually fold in flour mixture, about ½ cup at a time.

4. Gently transfer to an ungreased 10-in. tube pan. Cut through batter with a knife to remove air pockets. Bake on lowest oven rack until top springs back when lightly touched and cracks feel dry, 40-50 minutes. Immediately invert pan; cool completely in pan, about 1 hour.

5. Run a knife around sides and center tube of pan. Remove cake to a serving plate. For glaze, in a microwave, melt the chocolate chips with cream; stir until smooth. Drizzle over cake.

1 SLICE: 235 cal., 3g fat (2g sat. fat), 2mg chol., 102mg sod., 49g carb. (37g sugars, 1g fiber), 5g pro.

RUSTIC CARAMEL APPLE TART

Like an apple pie without the pan, this most scrumptious tart has a crispy crust
that cuts nicely and a yummy caramel topping everyone adores.

—Betty Fulks, Onia, AR

PREP: 20 MIN. + CHILLING • **BAKE:** 25 MIN. • **MAKES:** 4 SERVINGS

⅔ cup all-purpose flour
1 Tbsp. sugar
⅛ tsp. salt
¼ cup cold butter, cubed
6½ tsp. cold water
⅛ tsp. vanilla extract

FILLING
1½ cups chopped peeled
    tart apples
3 Tbsp. sugar
1 Tbsp. all-purpose flour

TOPPING
1 tsp. sugar
¼ tsp. ground cinnamon
1 large egg
1 Tbsp. water
2 Tbsp. caramel ice cream
    topping, warmed

1. In a large bowl, combine flour, sugar and salt; cut in butter until crumbly. Gradually add water and vanilla, tossing with a fork until dough forms a ball. Cover and refrigerate 30 minutes or until easy to handle.

2. Preheat oven to 400°. On a lightly floured surface, roll dough into a 10-in. circle. Transfer to a parchment-lined baking sheet. Combine the filling ingredients; spoon over crust to within 2 in. of the edges. Fold up edges of crust over filling, leaving center uncovered. Combine sugar and cinnamon; sprinkle over filling. Whisk egg and water; brush over crust.

3. Bake 25-30 minutes or until crust is golden and filling is bubbly. Using parchment, slide tart onto a wire rack. Drizzle with caramel topping. Serve warm.

1 SLICE: 298 cal., 13g fat (8g sat. fat), 77mg chol., 218mg sod., 42g carb. (24g sugars, 1g fiber), 4g pro.

BLUE
RIBBON
WINNER

BROWN SUGAR POUND CAKE

This tender pound cake is the first one I mastered. You'll want to eat the browned butter icing by the spoonful. It tastes just like pralines.

—Shawn Barto, Winter Garden, FL

PREP: 20 MIN. • BAKE: 55 MIN. + COOLING • MAKES: 16 SERVINGS

1½ cups unsalted
    butter, softened
2¼ cups packed brown sugar
5   large eggs, room
    temperature
2   tsp. vanilla extract
3   cups all-purpose flour
1   tsp. baking powder
¼   tsp. salt
1   cup sour cream

GLAZE
3   Tbsp. unsalted butter
¼   cup chopped pecans
1   cup confectioners' sugar
¼   tsp. vanilla extract
    Dash salt
2   to 3 Tbsp. half-
    and-half cream

1. Preheat oven to 350°. Grease and flour a 10-in. fluted tube pan.

2. Cream the butter and brown sugar until light and fluffy, 5-7 minutes. Add 1 egg at a time, beating well after each addition. Beat in vanilla. In another bowl, whisk flour, baking powder and salt; add to creamed mixture alternately with sour cream, beating after each addition just until combined.

3. Transfer to prepared pan. Bake until a toothpick inserted in center comes out clean, 55-65 minutes. Cool in pan 10 minutes before removing to a wire rack to cool completely.

4. For glaze, combine butter and pecans in a small saucepan over medium heat, stirring constantly, until the butter is light golden brown, 4-5 minutes. Stir into confectioners' sugar. Add vanilla, salt and enough cream to reach a drizzling consistency. Drizzle glaze over cake, allowing some to drip down sides. Let stand until set.

1 SLICE: 473 cal., 25g fat (15g sat. fat), 121mg chol., 193mg sod., 57g carb. (38g sugars, 1g fiber), 5g pro.

KITCHEN TIP: To remove cakes easily, use solid shortening to grease plain and fluted tube pans.

BEST STRAWBERRY SHORTCAKE

For a dazzling summer dessert, you can't beat juicy strawberries and fresh whipped cream over homemade shortcake. My father added even more indulgence by buttering the shortcake!

—Shirley Joan Helfenbein, Lapeer, MI

PREP: 15 MIN. • BAKE: 15 MIN. + COOLING • MAKES: 4 SERVINGS

1 cup all-purpose flour
1 Tbsp. sugar
1½ tsp. baking powder
¼ tsp. salt
¼ cup plus 2 tsp. cold butter, divided
1 large egg, room temperature
⅓ cup half-and-half cream
½ cup heavy whipping cream
1 Tbsp. confectioners' sugar
⅛ tsp. vanilla extract
2 cups fresh strawberries, sliced

1. In a small bowl, combine the flour, sugar, baking powder and salt. Cut in ¼ cup butter until the mixture resembles coarse crumbs. In a small bowl, combine egg and half-and-half; stir into crumb mixture just until moistened.

2. Spread the batter into a 6-in. round baking pan coated with cooking spray, slightly building up the edges. Bake at 450° for 13-15 minutes or until golden. Cool for 10 minutes before removing from pan to a wire rack.

3. In a small bowl, beat whipping cream, confectioners' sugar and vanilla until soft peaks form. Cut cake horizontally in half. Soften remaining butter. Place bottom layer on a serving plate; spread with butter. Top with half of strawberries and cream mixture. Repeat layers of cake, strawberries and cream.

1 SLICE: 420 cal., 28g fat (17g sat. fat), 140mg chol., 471mg sod., 36g carb. (10g sugars, 2g fiber), 7g pro.

THE VIEW FROM HERE
"My grandpa and his two brothers run our family farm, where we grow corn, soybeans and brome grass. I took this picture while shredding a path on our Farmall 460, on top of a bluff facing the Platte River."
—Cody Vyhlidal, Fremont, Nebraska

FROM TOP:

KITTY ON THE CASE
"My sister Becky took this little guy's photo on her ranch in Ontario, Canada. The cool kitty helps her keep the mouse population down."

—*Brenda Hansen, Clintonville, Wisconsin*

LOOKING AHEAD
"It was the golden hour at Double B Acres, and I was walking the fields with Dad. Like so many other farmers, my dad cares deeply for the land and his family. He is always watching over us and looking toward the future."

—*Megan Besancon, Sterling, Ohio*

MOCHA TRUFFLE CHEESECAKE

I went through a phase when I couldn't get enough cheesecake or coffee, so I created this rich dessert. It's ideal for get-togethers because it can be made in advance.

—Shannon Dormady, Great Falls, MT

PREP: 20 MIN. • BAKE: 50 MIN. + CHILLING • MAKES: 16 SERVINGS

1 pkg. devil's food cake mix (regular size)
6 Tbsp. butter, melted
1 large egg, room temperature
1 to 3 Tbsp. instant coffee granules

FILLING/TOPPING
2 pkg. (8 oz. each) cream cheese, softened
1 can (14 oz.) sweetened condensed milk
2 cups semisweet chocolate chips, melted and cooled
3 to 6 Tbsp. instant coffee granules
¼ cup hot water
3 large eggs, room temperature, lightly beaten
1 cup heavy whipping cream
¼ cup confectioners' sugar
⅓ tsp. almond extract
1 Tbsp. baking cocoa, optional

1. In a large bowl, combine the cake mix, butter, egg and coffee granules until well blended. Press onto the bottom and 2 in. up the sides of a greased 10-in. springform pan.

2. In another large bowl, beat cream cheese until smooth. Beat in milk and melted chips. Dissolve coffee granules in water; add to cream cheese mixture. Add eggs; beat on low speed just until combined. Pour into crust. Place pan on a baking sheet.

3. Bake at 325° until center is almost set, 50-55 minutes. Cool on a wire rack for 10 minutes. Carefully run a knife around edge of pan to loosen; cool 1 hour longer. Chill overnight.

4. Just before serving, in a large bowl, beat cream until soft peaks form. Beat in sugar and extract until stiff peaks form. Spread over top of cheesecake. Sprinkle with cocoa if desired. Refrigerate leftovers.

1 SLICE: 484 cal., 28g fat (16g sat. fat), 109mg chol., 309mg sod., 55g carb. (41g sugars, 2g fiber), 7g pro.

BLUE RIBBON WINNER

BANANA CREAM PIE

Made from our farm-fresh dairy products, this pie was a sensational creamy treat any time
Mom served it. Her recipe is a real treasure, and I've never found one that tastes better!

—Bernice Morris, Marshfield, MO

PREP: 20 MIN. + COOLING • MAKES: 8 SERVINGS

¾ cup sugar
⅓ cup all-purpose flour
¼ tsp. salt
2 cups whole milk
3 large egg yolks,
   room temperature,
   lightly beaten
2 Tbsp. butter
1 tsp. vanilla extract
3 medium, firm bananas
1 pastry shell (9 in.), baked
   Optional: Whipped cream
   and additional sliced
   bananas

1. In a saucepan, combine sugar, flour and salt; stir in milk and mix well. Cook over medium-high heat until the mixture is thickened and bubbly. Cook and stir for 2 minutes longer. Remove from the heat. Stir a small amount into egg yolks; return all to saucepan. Bring to a gentle boil. Cook and stir 2 minutes; remove from the heat. Add the butter and vanilla; cool slightly.

2. Slice bananas into crust; pour filling over top. Cool on wire rack for 1 hour. Store in the refrigerator. If desired, before serving, garnish with whipped cream and bananas.

1 SLICE: 338 cal., 14g fat (7g sat. fat), 101mg chol., 236mg sod., 49g carb. (30g sugars, 1g fiber), 5g pro.

KITCHEN TIP: To ensure a smooth, lump-free filling, stir sugar mixture constantly during cooking, and scrape the sides and bottom of the saucepan with a heatproof rubber spatula.

RECIPE INDEX